BANGKOK
TRAVEL GUIDE
2024

THE ULTIMATE TRAVEL GUIDE OF BANGKOK

ADAM W. GIBSON

BANGKOK TRAVEL GUIDE 2024
The Ultimate Travel Guide of Bangkok.

© Adam W. Gibson
© E.G.P. Editorial

Printed in USA.
ISBN-13: 9798390402948

BANGKOK
TRAVEL GUIDE 2024

THE MOST POPULAR PLACES IN BANGKOK

Bangkok, the vibrant capital of Thailand, boasts a wealth of diverse attractions that never cease to enthrall travelers. From bustling street markets to serene temples, this city is a melting pot of culture, history, and modernity.

The book, explores the city's must-see destinations, including intriguing museums, lively theaters, and captivating galleries. For those seeking adventure, the book offers a range of tours, walks, and activities that are perfect for kids. Food lovers will relish the recommendations for delectable restaurants, while nightlife enthusiasts will revel in the city's electric atmosphere.

The book is a comprehensive guide to Bangkok's most popular places, providing insider tips, detailed descriptions, and expert recommendations.
Whether you are a first-time visitor or a seasoned traveler, this book is the perfect companion to help you experience the best of what this city has to offer.

Happy travels!

TABLE OF CONTENTS

ATTRACTIONS

WAT PHRA KAEW & THE GRAND PALACE

Address: Na Phra Lan Road, Phra Nakhon, Bangkok, Thailand.

Historical background: Wat Phra Kaew and the Grand Palace are located in the heart of Bangkok and are considered to be the most sacred temple and palace in Thailand. The temple was built in the late 18th century and has been the center of Thai Buddhism for over 200 years. The Grand Palace was built in 1782 and served as the residence of the Kings of Siam and Thailand until 1925.

Practical information: Visitors are required to dress modestly and cover their knees and shoulders. The temple and palace are open daily from 8:30 AM to 3:30 PM, except on special religious holidays.

Highlights and must-sees: The highlight of Wat Phra Kaew is the Emerald Buddha, a highly revered statue of the Buddha made of green jade. The Grand Palace is a must-see for its stunning architecture and intricate decoration.

Cost: The entrance fee for Wat Phra Kaew and the Grand Palace is 500 THB.

Quality: The quality of the temple and palace is exceptional, with intricate details and stunning architecture.

Curiosity and facts: The Emerald Buddha is considered to be the most important religious artifact in Thailand

and is said to bring good luck and prosperity to the country.

Advice: Visitors should be respectful and observe the dress code, as well as not touch or point at any religious artifacts.

Getting there: The temple and palace are easily accessible by taxi, tuk-tuk, or the Chao Phraya Express Boat.

Nearby attractions: Wat Pho, the National Museum, and Wat MangkonKamalawat are all nearby and can be visited in a half-day trip.

WAT ARUN

Address: 158 Thanon Wang Doem, Wat Arun, Phra Nakhon, Bangkok, Thailand.

Historical background: Wat Arun, also known as the Temple of Dawn, is a Buddhist temple located on the west bank of the Chao Phraya River. It was built in the 17th century and is one of the most recognizable landmarks in Bangkok.

Practical information: The temple is open daily from 8:00 AM to 5:30 PM. Visitors are required to dress modestly and cover their knees and shoulders.

Highlights and must-sees: The highlight of Wat Arun is its stunning Khmer-style towers, which are covered in colorful glass and Chinese porcelain. The temple also offers great views of the river and the city.

Cost: The entrance fee for Wat Arun is 50 TH

Quality: The quality of the temple is exceptional, with intricate details and stunning decoration.

Curiosity and facts: Wat Arun is one of the oldest temples in Bangkok and is said to be a symbol of hope and renewal. The temple's name, "Temple of Dawn," reflects the belief that the morning light brings new hope and a fresh start.

Advice: Visitors should be respectful and observe the dress code, as well as not touch or point at any religious artifacts.

Getting there: Wat Arun can be easily reached by taxi, tuk-tuk, or the Chao Phraya Express Boat.

Nearby attractions: Wat Pho, Wat MangkonKamalawat, and the Royal Barges Museum are all nearby and can be visited in a half-day trip.

CHATUCHAK WEEKEND MARKET

Address: Kamphaeng Phet 2 Rd, Chatuchak, Bangkok, Thailand.

Historical background: Chatuchak Weekend Market is one of the largest outdoor markets in the world and has been in operation since the 1940s. It is a popular destination for both locals and tourists, offering a wide variety of goods and services.

Practical information: The market is only open on weekends from 9:00 AM to 6:00 PM. Visitors should be prepared for crowds and to haggle for prices.

Highlights and must-sees: The highlight of Chatuchak Weekend Market is the sheer variety of goods available, from clothing and accessories to furniture and home goods. Food stalls are also a must-see, offering a wide range of Thai and international cuisine.

Cost: There is no entrance fee for Chatuchak Weekend Market, but visitors should be prepared to spend money on purchases.

Quality: The quality of goods at the market can vary, but visitors can find high-quality items if they take the time to look.

Curiosity and facts: Chatuchak Weekend Market covers over 27 acres and has over 15,000 stalls, making it one of the largest markets in the world.

Advice: Visitors should be prepared for crowds and bring comfortable walking shoes, as well as a map or a guide to navigate the market.

Getting there: Chatuchak Weekend Market can be easily reached by taxi, tuk-tuk, or the BTS Skytrain.

Nearby attractions: The Chatuchak Park, the Museum of Siam, and the Wat MangkonKamalawat are all nearby and can be visited in a half-day trip.

WAT PHO

Address: 2 San Chao Pho Sua, Wat PhraChetuphon, Phra Nakhon, Bangkok, Thailand.

Historical background: Wat Pho, also known as the Temple of the Reclining Buddha, is a Buddhist temple located in the Phra Nakhon district of Bangkok. It was built in the 16th century and is one of the largest and oldest temples in the city.

Practical information: The temple is open daily from 8:00 AM to 5:00 PM. Visitors are required to dress modestly and cover their knees and shoulders.

Highlights and must-sees: The highlight of Wat Pho is the 46-meter long Reclining Buddha statue, which is covered in gold leaf and considered to be one of the largest reclining Buddha statues in the world. The temple also features beautiful architecture and a traditional Thai massage school.

Cost: The entrance fee for Wat Pho is 100 THB.

Quality: The quality of the temple is exceptional, with intricate details and stunning decoration.

Curiosity and facts: Wat Pho is known as the birthplace of traditional Thai massage and has been a center for health and wellness for over 200 years.

Advice: Visitors should be respectful and observe the dress code, as well as not touch or point at any religious artifacts.

Getting there: Wat Pho can be easily reached by taxi, tuk-tuk, or the Chao Phraya Express Boat.

Nearby attractions: Wat Arun, the Wat MangkonKamalawat, and the National Museum are all nearby and can be visited in a half-day trip.

KHAO SAN ROAD

Address: Khao San Road, Phra Nakhon, Bangkok, Thailand.

Historical background: Khao San Road is a bustling street located in the Phra Nakhon district of Bangkok. It is a popular destination for backpackers and budget travelers, offering a wide range of accommodation, dining, and shopping options.

Practical information: Khao San Road is accessible 24 hours a day and is always bustling with activity. Visitors should be prepared for crowds and to haggle for prices.

Highlights and must-sees: The highlight of Khao San Road is the lively atmosphere and the opportunity to experience Bangkok's vibrant nightlife. Street food stalls and local markets are also a must-see, offering a wide range of Thai and international cuisine.

Cost: There is no entrance fee for Khao San Road, but visitors should be prepared to spend money on food, shopping, and activities.

Quality: The quality of goods and services on Khao San Road can vary, but visitors can find high-quality options if they take the time to look.

Curiosity and facts: Khao San Road has been a popular destination for backpackers since the 1970s and has become known as the "backpacker capital of the world."

Advice: Visitors should be prepared for crowds and bring comfortable walking shoes, as well as be cautious of pickpocketing and scams in the area.

Getting there: Khao San Road can be easily reached by taxi, tuk-tuk, or the BTS Skytrain.

Nearby attractions: Wat Phra Kaew and the Grand Palace, Wat Pho, and the National Museum are all nearby and can be visited in a half-day trip.

JIM THOMPSON HOUSE

Address: 6 Soi Kasemsan 2, Rama I Rd, Wang Mai, Pathum Wan, Bangkok, Thailand.

Historical background: Jim Thompson House is a museum located in the heart of Bangkok, showcasing the life and work of American businessman and architect Jim Thompson. Thompson was a major figure in the revival of the Thai silk industry in the mid-20th century.

Practical information: The museum is open daily from 9:00 AM to 5:00 PM. Visitors are required to remove their shoes before entering the museum.

Highlights and must-sees: The highlight of Jim Thompson House is the opportunity to learn about Thompson's life and his impact on the Thai silk industry. The museum also showcases a beautiful collection of traditional Thai architecture and decoration.

Cost: The entrance fee for Jim Thompson House is 200 THB.

Quality: The quality of the museum is exceptional, with a well-curated collection and informative exhibits.

Curiosity and facts: Jim Thompson disappeared while on a trip in the Cameron Highlands of Malaysia in 1967 and was never found. His disappearance remains one of the most famous unsolved cases in Southeast Asian history.

Advice: Visitors should be prepared to remove their shoes before entering the museum and to follow the museum's rules and guidelines.

Getting there: Jim Thompson House can be easily reached by taxi, tuk-tuk, or the BTS Skytrain.

Nearby attractions: Wat MangkonKamalawat, Wat Phra Kaew and the Grand Palace, and the National Museum are all nearby and can be visited in a half-day trip.

SIAM PARAGON SHOPPING MALL

Address: 991/1 Rama I Rd, Khwaeng Pathum Wan, Khet Pathum Wan, Krung Thep Maha Nakhon 10330, Thailand.

Historical background: Siam Paragon Shopping Mall is a large shopping center located in the heart of Bangkok, offering a wide range of shopping, dining, and entertainment options.

Practical information: The mall is open daily from 10:00 AM to 10:00 PM. Visitors should be prepared to spend money on shopping and dining.

Highlights and must-sees: The highlight of Siam Paragon is the wide range of luxury shopping options, including high-end fashion brands and high-quality souvenirs. The mall also features a large food court, movie theaters, and a variety of entertainment options.

Cost: There is no entrance fee for Siam Paragon Shopping Mall, but visitors should be prepared to spend money on shopping and dining.

Quality: The quality of the mall is exceptional, with a well-maintained and clean environment, as well as high-quality shopping and dining options.

Curiosity and facts: Siam Paragon is one of the largest shopping malls in Southeast Asia and is considered to be one of the best shopping destinations in Bangkok.

Advice: Visitors should be prepared to spend money on shopping and dining and to bring comfortable walking shoes, as the mall is quite large.

Getting there: Siam Paragon Shopping Mall can be easily reached by taxi, tuk-tuk, or the BTS Skytrain.

Nearby attractions: Wat Phra Kaew and the Grand Palace, Wat Arun, and the Jim Thompson House are all nearby and can be visited in a half-day trip.

WAT SAKET

Address: 344 Thanon Bamrung Mueang, Phra Nakhon, Bangkok, Thailand.

Historical background: Wat Saket, also known as the Golden Mount Temple, is a Buddhist temple located in the Phra Nakhon district of Bangkok. It was built in the 14th century and is known for its golden chedi, which houses a relic of the Buddha.

Practical information: The temple is open daily from 8:00 AM to 5:00 PM. Visitors are required to dress modestly and cover their knees and shoulders.

Highlights and must-sees: The highlight of Wat Saket is the golden chedi, which provides stunning views of the city from its summit. The temple also features beautiful architecture and a peaceful atmosphere.

Cost: The entrance fee for Wat Saket is 50 THB.

Quality: The quality of the temple is exceptional, with intricate details and stunning decoration.

Curiosity and facts: Wat Saket has been a center of Buddhist worship for over 700 years and is one of the oldest temples in Bangkok.

Advice: Visitors should be respectful and observe the dress code, as well as not touch or point at any religious artifacts.

Getting there: Wat Saket can be easily reached by taxi, tuk-tuk, or the BTS Skytrain.

Nearby attractions: Wat Phra Kaew and the Grand Palace, Wat Pho, and the Royal Palace are all nearby and can be visited in a half-day trip.

ASIATIQUE THE RIVERFRONT

Address: 2194 Charoen Krung Rd, Wat Phraya Krai, Bang Kho Laem, Bangkok, Thailand.

Historical background: Asiatique The Riverfront is a large outdoor shopping and dining complex located on the banks of the Chao Phraya River in Bangkok. It features a wide range of shopping, dining, and entertainment options, including street food stalls, local markets, and cultural performances.

Practical information: The complex is open daily from 4:00 PM to 12:00 AM. Visitors should be prepared to spend money on shopping and dining.

Highlights and must-sees: The highlight of Asiatique The Riverfront is the opportunity to experience Bangkok's street food and local markets, as well as enjoy cultural performances and shows. The complex also features a wide range of shopping options, including local souvenirs and handicrafts.

Cost: There is no entrance fee for Asiatique The Riverfront, but visitors should be prepared to spend money on shopping and dining.

Quality: The quality of the complex is exceptional, with a well-maintained and clean environment, as well as high-quality shopping and dining options.

Curiosity and facts: Asiatique The Riverfront was established in 2012 and has become one of the most popular shopping and dining destinations in Bangkok.

Advice: Visitors should be prepared to spend money on shopping and dining and to bring comfortable walking shoes, as the complex is quite large.

Getting there: Asiatique The Riverfront can be easily reached by taxi, tuk-tuk, or the Chao Phraya Express Boat.

Nearby attractions: Wat Pho, Wat Arun, and the Grand Palace are all nearby and can be visited in a half-day trip.

MBK CENTER

Address: 444 Phayathai Rd, Wang Mai, Pathum Wan, Bangkok, Thailand.

Historical background: MBK Center is a large shopping mall located in the heart of Bangkok, offering a wide range of shopping, dining, and entertainment options.

Practical information: The mall is open daily from 10:00 AM to 10:00 PM. Visitors should be prepared to spend money on shopping and dining.

Highlights and must-sees: The highlight of MBK Center is the wide range of shopping options, including local souvenirs and electronics. The mall also features a large food court, movie theaters, and a variety of entertainment options.

Cost: There is no entrance fee for MBK Center, but visitors should be prepared to spend money on shopping and dining.

Quality: The quality of the mall is good, with a well-maintained and clean environment, as well as a variety of shopping and dining options.

Curiosity and facts: MBK Center is one of the largest shopping malls in Bangkok and is a popular destination for both locals and tourists.

Advice: Visitors should be prepared to spend money on shopping and dining and to bring comfortable walking shoes, as the mall is quite large.

Getting there: MBK Center can be easily reached by taxi, tuk-tuk, or the BTS Skytrain.

Nearby attractions: Wat Phra Kaew and the Grand Palace, Wat Arun, and the National Museum are all nearby and can be visited in a half-day trip.

SHOPS

MBK CENTER

Address: 444 Phaya Thai Rd, Wang Thong Lang, Bangkok 10330, Thailand

Phone: +66 2 620 9999

Products: MBK Center is a shopping mall that sells a wide range of products including electronics, clothing, accessories, and more.

Hours of operation: MBK Center is open daily from 10:00 AM to 10:00 PM.

Cost score: MBK Center is considered a budget-friendly shopping destination, with prices ranging from $ to $$.

Historical background: MBK Center was opened in 1985 and is one of the oldest shopping malls in Bangkok. It has become a popular tourist destination, attracting visitors from all over the world.

Highlights and must-sees: Some of the highlights of MBK Center include the numerous electronics and mobile phone shops, as well as the clothing and accessories stalls. Be sure to check out the food court on the top floor for a wide range of Thai and international cuisine.

Curiosity and facts: MBK Centeris one of the largest shopping malls in Bangkok, with over 2,000 shops spread over eight floors.

Advice: MBK Center can be quite crowded, especially on weekends, so be prepared for a busy shopping experience. It is also a good idea to negotiate prices with the vendors, as they are often willing to lower their prices for tourists.

Getting there: MBK Center is located near the National Stadium BTS Skytrain Station. From there, it is a short walk to the shopping mall.

Nearby attractions: Some of the nearby attractions include Siam Square, the Siam Center shopping mall, and the Jim Thompson House Museum.

CHATUCHAK WEEKEND MARKET

Address: Kamphaeng Phet 2 Rd, Chatuchak, Bangkok 10900, Thailand

Phone: +66 2 272 4334

Products: Chatuchak Weekend Market is a massive outdoor market that sells a wide range of products including clothing, accessories, home goods, and more.

Hours of operation: Chatuchak Weekend Market is only open on weekends from 9:00 AM to 6:00 PM.

Cost score: Chatuchak Weekend Market is considered a budget-friendly shopping destination, with prices ranging from $ to $$.

Historical background: Chatuchak Weekend Market has been operating since the 1940s and is one of the largest outdoor markets in the world. It is a popular destination for both locals and tourists alike.

Highlights and must-sees: Some of the highlights of Chatuchak Weekend Market include the wide variety of street food stalls, the handmade goods and crafts, and the clothing and accessories stalls. Be sure to try some of the Thai street food and haggle with the vendors for the best prices.

Curiosity and facts: Chatuchak Weekend Market has over 15,000 stalls and is spread over 35 acres, making it one of the largest outdoor markets in the world.

Advice: Chatuchak Weekend Market can be quite crowded, especially on weekends, so be prepared for a busy shopping experience. It is also a good idea to bring cash and wear comfortable shoes, as the market can be quite large and tiring to navigate.

Getting there: Chatuchak Weekend Market is located near the Chatuchak Park MRT Station. From there, it is a short walk to the market.

Nearby attractions: Some of the nearby attractions include the Chatuchak Park, the Chatuchak Art Center, and the Or Tor Kor Market.

CENTRAL WORLD

Address: 999/9 Rama I Rd, Pathum Wan, Bangkok 10330, Thailand

Phone: +66 2 100 1234

Products: Central World is a shopping mall that sells a wide range of products including clothing, accessories, electronics, and more.

Hours of operation: Central World is open daily from 10:00 AM to 10:00 PM.

Cost score: Central World is considered a mid-range shopping destination, with prices ranging from $$ to $$$.

Historical background: Central World was opened in 1990 and has become one of the largest shopping malls in Bangkok. It is a popular destination for both locals and tourists alike.

Highlights and must-sees: Some of the highlights of Central World include the numerous luxury clothing and accessory shops, the food court, and the rooftop garden. Be sure to check out the ice skating rink and the cinema on the top floor.

Curiosity and facts: Central World was the largest shopping mall in Southeast Asia until the opening of the larger Iconsiam shopping mall in 2018.

Advice: Central World can be quite crowded, especially on weekends, so be prepared for a busy shopping experience. It is also a good idea to bring cash and wear comfortable shoes, as the mall is quite large and tiring to navigate.

Getting there: Central World is located near the Chit Lom BTS Skytrain Station. From there, it is a short walk to the shopping mall.

Nearby attractions: Some of the nearby attractions include the Siam Paragon shopping mall, the Siam Center shopping mall, and the Jim Thompson House Museum.

SIAM PARAGON

Address: 991 Rama I Rd, Pathum Wan, Bangkok 10330, Thailand

Phone: +66 2 610 8000

Products: Siam Paragon is a luxury shopping mall that sells a wide range of high-end products including designer clothing, accessories, electronics, and more.

Hours of operation: Siam Paragon is open daily from 10:00 AM to 10:00 PM.

Cost score: Siam Paragon is considered a high-end shopping destination, with prices ranging from $$$ to $$$$.

Historical background: Siam Paragon was opened in 2005 and has become one of the largest and most popular luxury shopping malls in Bangkok. It is a popular destination for both locals and tourists alike.

Highlights and must-sees: Some of the highlights of Siam Paragon include the numerous luxury clothing and accessory shops, the food court, and the aquarium. Be sure to check out the luxury car showroom on the top floor and the cinema.

Curiosity and facts: Siam Paragon was voted as the second best shopping mall in the world by Travel + Leisure magazine in 2008.

Advice: Siam Paragon can be quite crowded, especially on weekends, so be prepared for a busy shopping experience. It is also a good idea to bring cash and wear comfortable shoes, as the mall is quite large and tiring to navigate.

Getting there: Siam Paragon is located near the Siam BTS Skytrain Station. From there, it is a short walk to the shopping mall.

Nearby attractions: Some of the nearby attractions include the Central World shopping mall, the Siam Center shopping mall, and the Jim Thompson House Museum.

TERMINAL 21

Address: 88 Soi Sukhumvit 19, Khwaeng Khlong Toei Nuea, Khet Watthana, Bangkok 10110, Thailand

Phone: +66 2 108 0888

Products: Terminal 21 is a shopping mall that sells a wide range of products including clothing, accessories, electronics, and more.

Hours of operation: Terminal 21 is open daily from 10:00 AM to 10:00 PM.

Cost score: Terminal 21 is considered a mid-range shopping destination, with prices ranging from $$ to $$$.

Historical background: Terminal 21 was opened in 2011 and has become a popular shopping destination in Bangkok. It is known for its unique design, which is modeled after an airport terminal.

Highlights and must-sees: Some of the highlights of Terminal 21 include its unique design, the food court, and the themed floors that are modeled after different cities around the world. Be sure to check out the cinema and the rooftop garden.

Curiosity and facts: Terminal 21 is one of the largest shopping malls in Bangkok and is known for its unique design and themed floors.

Advice: Terminal 21 can be quite crowded, especially on weekends, so be prepared for a busy shopping experience. It is also a good idea to bring cash and wear comfortable shoes, as the mall is quite large and tiring to navigate.

Getting there: Terminal 21 is located near the Asok BTS Skytrain Station. From there, it is a short walk to the shopping mall.

Nearby attractions: Some of the nearby attractions include the Soi Cowboy nightlife area, the Terminal 21 shopping mall, and the Queen Sirikit National Convention Center.

THE PLATINUM FASHION MALL

Address: 222 Phetchaburi Rd, Ratchathewi, Bangkok 10400, Thailand

Phone: +66 2 247 5933

Products: The Platinum Fashion Mall is a wholesale clothing market that sells a wide range of clothing and accessories at wholesale prices.

Hours of operation: The Platinum Fashion Mall is open daily from 9:30 AM to 6:00 PM.

Cost score: The Platinum Fashion Mall is considered a budget-friendly shopping destination, with prices ranging from $ to $$.

Historical background: The Platinum Fashion Mall was opened in 2006 and has become a popular shopping destination for both locals and tourists who are looking for wholesale clothing and accessories.

Highlights and must-sees: Some of the highlights of The Platinum Fashion Mall include the numerous clothing and accessory stalls, the food court, and the wide variety of styles and designs available. Be sure to negotiate prices with the vendors, as they are often willing to lower their prices for tourists.

Curiosity and facts: The Platinum Fashion Mall is one of the largest wholesale clothing markets in Bangkok and is known for its low prices and wide selection of styles and designs.

Advice: The Platinum Fashion Mall can be quite crowded, especially on weekends, so be prepared for a busy shopping experience. It is also a good idea to bring cash and wear comfortable shoes, as the market can be quite large and tiring to navigate.

Getting there: The Platinum Fashion Mall is located near the Ratchathewi BTS Skytrain Station. From there, it is a short walk to the shopping mall.

Nearby attractions: Some of the nearby attractions include the Siam Square shopping area, the Central World shopping mall, and the Pratunam Market.

PANTIP PLAZA

Address: 604/3 Phetchaburi Rd, ThanonPhaya Thai, Ratchathewi, Bangkok 10400, Thailand

Phone: +66 2 615 0555

Products: Pantip Plaza is a shopping mall that specializes in electronics and computer equipment. It also sells a wide range of products including clothing, accessories, and more.

Hours of operation: Pantip Plaza is open daily from 10:00 AM to 8:00 PM.

Cost score: Pantip Plaza is considered a budget-friendly shopping destination, with prices ranging from $ to $$.

Historical background: Pantip Plaza was opened in the 1980s and has become a popular shopping destination for electronics and computer equipment in Bangkok. It is also known for its low prices and wide selection of products.

Highlights and must-sees: Some of the highlights of Pantip Plaza include the numerous electronics stalls, the food court, and the computer repair shops. Be sure to negotiate prices with the vendors, as they are often willing to lower their prices for tourists.

Curiosity and facts: Pantip Plaza is one of the largest electronics markets in Bangkok and is known for its low prices and wide selection of products.

Advice: Pantip Plaza can be quite crowded, especially on weekends, so be prepared for a busy shopping experience. It is also a good idea to bring cash and wear comfortable shoes, as the market can be quite large and tiring to navigate.

Getting there: Pantip Plaza is located near the Ratchathewi BTS Skytrain Station. From there, it is a short walk to the shopping mall.

Nearby attractions: Some of the nearby attractions include the Siam Square shopping area, the Central World shopping mall, and the Pratunam Market.

THE EMPORIUM

Address: 622 Sukhumvit Rd, Khlong Tan Nuea, Watthana, Bangkok 10110, Thailand.

Phone: +66 2 269 1000.

Products: Luxury fashion, jewelry, beauty products, and home decor.

Hours of operation: 10:00 AM to 10:00 PM daily.

Cost score: $$ - $$$.

Historical background: The Emporium is one of Bangkok's most popular luxury shopping centers, known for its high-end fashion, jewelry, beauty products, and home decor. It was opened in 1997 and has since become a must-visit destination for shoppers looking for the best of the best in Bangkok.

Highlights and must-sees: The Emporium's highlights include a wide range of high-end fashion brands, as well as a beautiful jewelry section featuring both international and local brands. The beauty section is also a must-visit, with an array of skincare, makeup, and fragrance products from some of the world's best brands. The home decor section is also worth a visit, with a range of furniture, kitchenware, and home accessories to choose from.

Curiosity and facts: The Emporium is housed in a beautiful building with a sleek and modern design, and features a large, open-air atrium that provides plenty of natural light. The shopping center is also home to a number of restaurants, cafes, and bars, making it a great place to stop for a bite to eat or a drink after a day of shopping.

Advice: If you're looking for luxury shopping in Bangkok, The Emporium is a must-visit. Be prepared to spend a bit more here than at other shopping centers, but the quality of the products and the shopping experience make it well worth it.

Getting there: To get to The Emporium, take the BTS Skytrain to Phrom Phong Station. From there, it's a short walk to the shopping center.

Nearby attractions: Some nearby attractions include the Bangkok Art and Culture Centre, the Benjasiri Park, and the Soi Cowboy nightlife district.

CENTRAL EMBASSY

Address: 1031 Ploenchit Rd, Lumphini, Pathum Wan, Bangkok 10330, Thailand

Phone: +66 2 160 5600

Products: Central Embassy is a luxury shopping mall that sells a wide range of high-end products including designer clothing, accessories, electronics, and more.

Hours of operation: Central Embassy is open daily from 10:00 AM to 10:00 PM.

Cost score: Central Embassy is considered a high-end shopping destination, with prices ranging from $$$ to $$$$.

Historical background: Central Embassy was opened in 2014 and has quickly become one of the most popular luxury shopping malls in Bangkok. It is a popular destination for both locals and tourists alike.

Highlights and must-sees: Some of the highlights of Central Embassy include the numerous luxury clothing and accessory shops, the food court, and the art exhibitions. Be sure to check out the rooftop garden and the cinema.

Curiosity and facts: Central Embassy is the tallest building in Bangkok and is known for its unique architecture and high-end shopping experience.

Advice: Central Embassy can be quite crowded, especially on weekends, so be prepared for a busy shopping experience. It is also a good idea to bring cash and wear comfortable shoes, as the mall is quite large and tiring to navigate.

Getting there: Central Embassy is located near the Phloen Chit BTS Skytrain Station. From there, it is a short walk to the shopping mall.

Nearby attractions: Some of the nearby attractions include the Benjasiri Park, the Erawan Shrine, and the Central World shopping mall.

INDEX LIVING MALL

Address: 1522 Phahonyothin Rd, Chatuchak, Bangkok 10900, Thailand

Phone: +66 2 939 5555

Products: Index Living Mall is a shopping mall that specializes in furniture and home decor. It also sells a wide range of products including clothing, accessories, and more.

Hours of operation: Index Living Mall is open daily from 10:00 AM to 10:00 PM.

Cost score: Index Living Mall is considered a mid-range shopping destination, with prices ranging from $$ to $$$.

Historical background: Index Living Mall was established in the 1990s and has become a popular shopping destination for furniture and home decor in Bangkok. It is known for its wide selection of products and affordable prices.

Highlights and must-sees: Some of the highlights of Index Living Mall include the numerous furniture and home decor shops, the food court, and the wide variety of styles and designs available. Be sure to check out the home decor exhibitions and the furniture showrooms.

Curiosity and facts: Index Living Mall is one of the largest furniture and home decor markets in Bangkok and is known for its wide selection of products and affordable prices.

Advice: Index Living Mall can be quite crowded, especially on weekends, so be prepared for a busy shopping experience. It is also a good idea to bring cash and wear comfortable shoes, as the market can be quite large and tiring to navigate.

Getting there: Index Living Mall is located near the Chatuchak Park BTS Skytrain Station. From there, it is a short walk to the shopping mall.

Nearby attractions: Some of the nearby attractions include the Chatuchak Weekend Market, the Mo Chit Bus Terminal, and the Lat Phrao Night Bazaar.

MUSEUMS

THE NATIONAL MUSEUM BANGKOK

Address: Na Phrathat Road, Phra Nakhon, Bangkok 10200, Thailand.

Phone: +66 2 224 1333.

Exhibitions and collections: The National Museum Bangkok has a vast collection of Thai art and artifacts from the Sukhothai to the Rattanakosin periods. The museum showcases various styles of Thai architecture, sculptures, and Buddhist art.

Admission fees and hours of operation: Admission fee is 200 THB for adults and 100 THB for children. The museum is open from Wednesday to Sunday, 9:00 am to 4:00 pm.

Historical background: The National Museum Bangkok was established in 1874 and is the largest museum in Thailand. It houses a wide collection of Thai cultural and historical artifacts, which are valuable resources for the study of Thai art and culture.

Highlights and must-sees: Some of the must-see exhibits include the Sukhothai Buddha, the King Rama V Equestrian Statue, and the Ramakien Murals.

Curiosity and facts: The National Museum Bangkok was originally the palace of King Rama V and was later converted into a museum to showcase Thai art and cultural heritage.

Advice: Visitors are advised to allocate at least half a day to explore the museum and its collections. Wear comfortable shoes as the museum covers a large area.

Getting there: The National Museum Bangkok is located near the San Chao Pho Sua and the Wat MangkonKamalawat temples. From the metro station, take the MRT to the Hua Lamphong Station, then take a taxi to the museum.

Nearby attractions: Some of the nearby attractions include the Wat MangkonKamalawat, the Wat MangkonKamalawat, and the Wat MangkonKamalawat temples.

THE MUSEUM OF SIAM

Address: San Chao Pho Sua, Thanon San Chao Pho Sua, Phra Nakhon, Bangkok, Thailand.

Phone: +66 2 225 2777.

Exhibitions and collections: The Museum of Siam showcases the history and culture of Thailand, including the origins of the Thai people, the development of the Thai kingdom, and the cultural heritage of the Thai people.

Admission fees and hours of operation: Admission fee is 200 THB for adults and 100 THB for children. The museum is open from Tuesday to Sunday, 10:00 am to 5:00 pm.

Historical background: The Museum of Siam was established in 2005 to showcase the rich cultural heritage of Thailand. The museum is housed in a former royal palace and is one of the most popular cultural museums in Bangkok.

Highlights and must-sees: Some of the must-see exhibits include the interactive displays and exhibits on Thai culture and history, the Thai language and writing system, and the traditional Thai way of life.

Curiosity and facts: The Museum of Siam is the first museum in Thailand to use modern technology and multimedia displays to present the history and culture of Thailand.

Advice: Visitors are advised to allocate at least 2 hours to explore the museum and its collections. Wear comfortable shoes as the museum covers a large area.

Getting there: The Museum of Siam is located in the heart of Bangkok and is easily accessible by public transport. From the metro station, take the BTS to the Siam Station, then take a taxi to the museum.

Nearby attractions: Some of the nearby attractions include the Siam Square shopping district, the Siam Paragon shopping mall, and the CentralWorld shopping complex.

BANGKOK NATIONAL MUSEUM

Address: Na Phrathat Road, Phra Nakhon, Bangkok 10200, Thailand.

Phone: +66 2 224 1333.

Exhibitions and collections: The Bangkok National Museum has a vast collection of Thai art and artifacts from the Sukhothai to the Rattanakosin periods. The museum showcases various styles of Thai architecture, sculptures, and Buddhist art.

Admission fees and hours of operation: Admission fee is 200 THB for adults and 100 THB for children. The museum is open from Wednesday to Sunday, 9:00 am to 4:00 pm.

Historical background: The Bangkok National Museum was established in 1874 and is the largest museum in Thailand. It houses a wide collection of Thai cultural and historical artifacts, which are valuable resources for the study of Thai art and culture.

Highlights and must-sees: Some of the must-see exhibits include the Sukhothai Buddha, the King Rama V Equestrian Statue, and the Ramakien Murals.

Curiosity and facts: The Bangkok National Museum was originally the palace of King Rama V and was later converted into a museum to showcase Thai art and cultural heritage.

Advice: Visitors are advised to allocate at least half a day to explore the museum and its collections. Wear comfortable shoes as the museum covers a large area.

Getting there: The Bangkok National Museum is located near the San Chao Pho Sua and the Wat MangkonKamalawat temples. From the metro station, take the MRT to the Hua Lamphong Station, then take a taxi to the museum.

Nearby attractions: Some of the nearby attractions include the Wat MangkonKamalawat, the Wat MangkonKamalawat, and the Wat MangkonKamalawat temples, as well as the San Chao Pho Sua temple.

THE ROYAL BARGE NATIONAL MUSEUM

Address: Klongsan, Bangkok 10600, Thailand.

Phone: +66 2 437 6077.

Exhibitions and collections: The Royal Barge National Museum showcases the history and tradition of the Royal Barge Procession, which is a significant part of Thai cultural heritage. The museum also showcases various types of traditional Thai boats and barges.

Admission fees and hours of operation: Admission fee is 200 THB for adults and 100 THB for children. The museum is open from Tuesday to Sunday, 9:00 am to 4:00 pm.

Historical background: The Royal Barge National Museum was established in 1972 to preserve the traditions and cultural heritage of the Royal Barge Procession. The museum is located on the banks of the Chao Phraya River in Bangkok.

Highlights and must-sees: Some of the must-see exhibits include the various types of traditional Thai boats and barges, as well as the history and tradition of the Royal Barge Procession.

Curiosity and facts: The Royal Barge Procession is a significant part of Thai cultural heritage and is held only on special occasions, such as the coronation of a new king.

Advice: Visitors are advised to allocate at least 2 hours to explore the museum and its collections. Wear comfortable shoes as the museum covers a large area.

Getting there: The Royal Barge National Museum is located on the banks of the Chao Phraya River in Bangkok. From the metro station, take the MRT to the Hua Lamphong Station, then take a taxi to the museum.

Nearby attractions: Some of the nearby attractions include the Wat MangkonKamalawat, the Wat MangkonKamalawat, and the Wat MangkonKamalawat temples.

THE QUEEN'S GALLERY

Address: Chao Fa Road, Phra Nakhon, Bangkok 10200, Thailand.

Phone: +66 2 280 8184.

Exhibitions and collections: The Queen's Gallery showcases the art and cultural heritage of Thailand, including traditional Thai arts and crafts, textiles, and ceramics.

Admission fees and hours of operation: Admission fee is 200 THB for adults and 100 THB for children. The gallery is open from Tuesday to Sunday, 9:00 am to 4:00 pm.

Historical background: The Queen's Gallery was established in 1987 to showcase the art and cultural heritage of Thailand, with a focus on traditional Thai arts and crafts. The gallery is located in the heart of Bangkok and is a popular destination for both Thai and foreign visitors.

Highlights and must-sees: Some of the must-see exhibits include the traditional Thai textiles, ceramics, and other arts and crafts.

Curiosity and facts: The Queen's Gallery is a non-profit organization, with the goal of promoting and preserving the art and cultural heritage of Thailand.

Advice: Visitors are advised to allocate at least 2 hours to explore the gallery and its collections. Wear comfortable shoes as the gallery covers a large area.

Getting there: The Queen's Gallery is located in the heart of Bangkok and is easily accessible by public transport. From the metro station, take the BTS to the Siam Station, then take a taxi to the gallery.

Nearby attractions: Some of the nearby attractions include the Siam Square shopping district, the Siam Paragon shopping mall, and the CentralWorld shopping complex.

THE JIM THOMPSON HOUSE MUSEUM

Address: 6 Soi Kasemsan 2, Rama 1 Road, Wang Mai, Pathum Wan, Bangkok 10330, Thailand.

Phone: +66 2 216 7368.

Exhibitions and collections: The Jim Thompson House Museum showcases the life and work of American businessman and art collector Jim Thompson, as well as traditional Thai arts and architecture.

Admission fees and hours of operation: Admission fee is 200 THB for adults and 100 THB for children. The museum is open from Tuesday to Sunday, 9:00 am to 4:00 pm.

Historical background: The Jim Thompson House Museum is located in a traditional Thai-style house and was the residence of American businessman and art collector Jim Thompson. The house has been preserved as a museum to showcase the traditional Thai arts and architecture.

Highlights and must-sees: Some of the must-see exhibits include the traditional Thai-style house, the collection of Thai and Southeast Asian art, and the life and work of Jim Thompson.

Curiosity and facts: Jim Thompson was a prominent American businessman and art collector who played a major role in the revival of the Thai silk industry in the mid-20th century.

Advice: Visitors are advised to allocate at least 2 hours to explore the museum and its collections. Wear comfortable shoes as the museum covers a large area.

Getting there: The Jim Thompson House Museum is located in the heart of Bangkok and is easily accessible by public transport. From the metro station, take the BTS to the National Stadium Station, then take a taxi to the museum.

Nearby attractions: Some of the nearby attractions include the MBK shopping mall, the Siam Square shopping district, and the Siam Paragon shopping mall.

THE ANCIENT CITY

Address: Samut Prakan, Thailand.

Phone: +66 2 781 8888.

Exhibitions and collections: The Ancient City showcases the history and culture of Thailand, featuring replicas of various famous temples, palaces, and historical sites from all over the country.

Admission fees and hours of operation: Admission fee is 400 THB for adults and 200 THB for children. The museum is open daily, 9:00 am to 5:00 pm.

Historical background: The Ancient City is a large outdoor museum that was established to showcase the history and culture of Thailand through replicas of famous temples, palaces, and historical sites.

Highlights and must-sees: Some of the must-see exhibits include the replicas of the Wat Arun, the Wat Phra Kaew, and the Grand Palace in Bangkok.

Curiosity and facts: The Ancient City covers over 200 acres and is one of the largest outdoor museums in the world.

Advice: Visitors are advised to allocate at least half a day to explore the museum and its collections. Wear comfortable shoes as the museum covers a large area.

Getting there: The Ancient City is located in Samut Prakan, a province located just outside of Bangkok. From the metro station, take the BTS to the Mo Chit Station, then take a taxi to the museum.

Nearby attractions: Some of the nearby attractions include the Erawan Museum and the PhraPathom Chedi.

THE MUSEUM OF CONTEMPORARY ART

Address: ThanonRatchadaphisek, Huai Khwang, Bangkok 10310, Thailand.

Phone: +66 2 939 7052.

Exhibitions and collections: The Museum of Contemporary Art showcases contemporary art from Thailand and around the world. The museum features various forms of contemporary art, including paintings, sculptures, installations, and multimedia displays.

Admission fees and hours of operation: Admission fee is 200 THB for adults and 100 THB for children. The museum is open from Tuesday to Sunday, 9:00 am to 4:00 pm.

Historical background: The Museum of Contemporary Art was established to showcase contemporary art from Thailand and around the world. The museum is located in the heart of Bangkok and is a popular destination for art lovers.

Highlights and must-sees: Some of the must-see exhibits include the contemporary art from Thailand and around the world, as well as the multimedia displays and installations.

Curiosity and facts: The Museum of Contemporary Art is one of the leading institutions for contemporary art in Thailand and is known for its innovative exhibitions and programs.

Advice: Visitors are advised to allocate at least 2 hours to explore the museum and its collections. Wear comfortable shoes as the museum covers a large area.

Getting there: The Museum of Contemporary Art is located in the heart of Bangkok and is easily accessible by public transport. From the metro station, take the BTS to the Phra Ram 9 Station, then take a taxi to the museum.

Nearby attractions: Some of the nearby attractions include the Fortune Town shopping mall, the Esplanade shopping mall, and the CentralPlaza Rama 9 shopping complex.

THE KING PRAJADHIPOK MUSEUM

Address: Na Phra Lan Road, Phra Nakhon, Bangkok 10200, Thailand.

Phone: +66 2 281 7010.

Exhibitions and collections: The King Prajadhipok Museum showcases the life and reign of King Prajadhipok, the 7th king of Thailand. The museum also showcases the history of the Thai monarchy and the Thai constitutional monarchy.

Admission fees and hours of operation: Admission fee is 200 THB for adults and 100 THB for children. The museum is open from Tuesday to Sunday, 9:00 am to 4:00 pm.

Historical background: The King Prajadhipok Museum was established to showcase the life and reign of King Prajadhipok, the 7th king of Thailand. The museum is located in the heart of Bangkok and is a popular destination for history enthusiasts.

Highlights and must-sees: Some of the must-see exhibits include the history of the Thai monarchy and the reign of King Prajadhipok.

Curiosity and facts: King Prajadhipok was the 7th king of Thailand and played a significant role in the transition of Thailand from an absolute monarchy to a constitutional monarchy.

Advice: Visitors are advised to allocate at least 2 hours to explore the museum and its collections. Wear comfortable shoes as the museum covers a large area.

Getting there: The King Prajadhipok Museum is located in the heart of Bangkok and is easily accessible by public transport. From the metro station, take the BTS to the Siam Station, then take a taxi to the museum.

Nearby attractions: Some of the nearby attractions include the Siam Square shopping district, the Siam Paragon shopping mall, and the CentralWorld shopping complex.

THE BAN KAMTHIENG MUSEUM

Address: Soi 21, Thanon Sukhumvit, Watthana, Bangkok 10110, Thailand.

Phone: +662 258 6077.

Exhibitions and collections: The Ban Kamthieng Museum showcases the traditional culture and way of life of the northern Thai people, also known as the Lanna people. The museum features traditional Lanna houses, objects, and textiles.

Admission fees and hours of operation: Admission fee is 200 THB for adults and 100 THB for children. The museum is open from Tuesday to Sunday, 9:00 am to 4:00 pm.

Historical background: The Ban Kamthieng Museum is located in a traditional Lanna-style house and was established to showcase the traditional culture and way of life of the northern Thai people. The museum is a popular destination for those interested in the cultural heritage of Thailand.

Highlights and must-sees: Some of the must-see exhibits include the traditional Lanna-style house, the collection of Lanna textiles, and the traditional Lanna objects.

Curiosity and facts: The Lanna people are an ethnic group indigenous to northern Thailand and have a distinct culture, language, and traditions.

Advice: Visitors are advised to allocate at least 2 hours to explore the museum and its collections. Wear comfortable shoes as the museum covers a large area.

Getting there: The Ban Kamthieng Museum is located in Bangkok and is easily accessible by public transport. From the metro station, take the BTS to the Phrom Phong Station, then take a taxi to the museum.

Nearby attractions: Some of the nearby attractions include the EmQuartier shopping mall, the Emporium shopping mall, and the Benjasiri Park.

THEATERS

SIAM NIRAMIT

Address: 8 Tiam Ruammit Road, Khwaeng Hua Lam Phong, Khet Klong Toei, Bangkok 10110, Thailand.

Phone: +66 2204 1333

Performances and shows: Siam Niramit is a world-class cultural attraction that presents a spectacular show that takes you through the history, culture, and spiritual heritage of Thailand.

Ticket prices and availability: Ticket prices start at THB 1,200 and are available for purchase online or at the box office. Availability may vary based on the show schedule and holidays.

Show times: Shows typically start at 8:00 PM and run for approximately 90 minutes.

Historical background: Siam Niramit was established in 1998 and has been providing visitors with a unique and immersive cultural experience ever since.

Highlights and must-sees: The highlights of Siam Niramit include its stunning sets, costumes, and special effects, as well as its talented performers, who bring to life the rich cultural heritage of Thailand.

Curiosity and facts: Siam Niramitis the largest theater in Thailand and one of the largest in Southeast Asia, with a seating capacity of over 2,000 people.

Advice: Visitors are advised to arrive early to secure a good seat and to take advantage of the pre-show activities and exhibitions on offer.

Getting there: Siam Niramit is located near the Hua Lamphong MRT Station. Take Exit 2 and walk for approximately 5 minutes to reach the theater.

Nearby attractions: Some of the nearby attractions include Wat MangkonKamalawat, Wat MangkornKamalawas, and Wat MangkonKamalawat.

BAAN TALING CHAN FLOATING MARKET

Address: Taling Chan, Bangkok, Thailand.

Phone: +66 2436 6071

Performances and shows: Baan Taling Chan Floating Market is a traditional floating market that offers visitors a unique shopping experience and a glimpse into Thai culture and customs.

Ticket prices and availability: Admission to the market is free, but visitors should expect to pay for food and other items purchased at the market stalls.

Show times: The market is open daily from 9:00 AM to 5:00 PM.

Historical background: Baan Taling Chan Floating Market has a long history and has been a staple of Thai life for generations.

Highlights and must-sees: The highlights of the market include its colorful boats and stalls, its delicious local cuisine, and the chance to witness traditional Thai bargaining and bargaining practices.

Curiosity and facts: Baan Taling Chan is one of the few remaining floating markets in Thailand and is considered a must-visit for anyone interested in traditional Thai culture and lifestyle.

Advice: Visitors are advised to bring plenty of cash and to be prepared for a crowded and lively atmosphere.

Getting there: Baan Taling Chan Floating Market can be reached by taking the MRT to Taling Chan Station and then taking a taxi or local boat to the market.

Nearby attractions: Some of the nearby attractions include Wat Bang Phai, Wat Bang Nam Phueng Nok, and Wat Bang Nam Phueng Tai.

CALYPSO CABARET

Address: AsiatiqueThe Riverfront, 2194 Charoen Krung Road, Wat Phraya Krai, Bang Kho Laem, Bangkok 10120, Thailand.

Phone: +66 2108 4488

Performances and shows: Calypso Cabaret is a world-famous cabaret show that features a diverse cast of talented performers and stunning costumes and sets.

Ticket prices and availability: Ticket prices start at THB 1,100 and are available for purchase online or at the box office. Availability may vary based on the show schedule and holidays.

Show times: Shows typically start at 8:15 PM and run for approximately 90 minutes.

Historical background: Calypso Cabaret has been entertaining audiences for over 30 years and has established itself as one of the premier cabaret shows in Asia.

Highlights and must-sees: The highlights of Calypso Cabaret include its talented performers, stunning costumes, and elaborate sets, as well as its high-energy and highly entertaining performances.

Curiosity and facts: Calypso Cabaret is known for its stunning LED stage and state-of-the-art lighting and sound system, which provides a truly immersive experience for its audience.

Advice: Visitors are advised to arrive early to secure a good seat and to take advantage of the pre-show activities and exhibitions on offer.

Getting there: Calypso Cabaret is located at AsiatiqueThe Riverfront, which can be reached by taking the BTS Skytrain to SaphanTaksin Station and then taking a shuttle boat to Asiatique.

Nearby attractions: Some of the nearby attractions include Wat MangkornKamalawat, Wat MangkonKamalawas, and Wat MangkonKamalawat.

MAMBO CABARET

Address: 4 Soi Soonvijai 7, New Petchburi Road, Bangkapi, Huai Khwang, Bangkok 10310, Thailand.

Phone: +66 2118 7777

Performances and shows: Mambo Cabaret is a vibrant and entertaining cabaret show that features a talented cast of performers and stunning costumes and sets.

Ticket prices and availability: Ticket prices start at THB 1,000 and are available for purchase online or at the box office. Availability may vary based on the show schedule and holidays.

Show times: Shows typically start at 8:00 PM and run for approximately 90 minutes.

Historical background: Mambo Cabaret has been entertaining audiences for over 20 years and is considered one of the top cabaret shows in Bangkok.

Highlights and must-sees: The highlights of Mambo Cabaret include its talented performers, stunning costumes, and elaborate sets, as well as its high-energy and highly entertaining performances.

Curiosity and facts: Mambo Cabaret is known for its unique blend of Thai culture and modern entertainment, making it a must-see for anyone visiting Bangkok.

Advice: Visitors are advised to arrive early to secure a good seat and to take advantage of the pre-show activities and exhibitions on offer.

Getting there: Mambo Cabaret is located near the Petchaburi MRT Station. Take Exit 3 and walk for approximately 5 minutes to reach the theater.

Nearby attractions: Some of the nearby attractions include Wat MangkornKamalawat, Wat MangkonKamalawas, and Wat MangkonKamalawat.

THE STAGE

Address: 6th Floor, CentralWorld, Ratchadamri Road, Pathum Wan, Bangkok 10330, Thailand.

Phone: +66 2168 6888

Performances and shows: The Stage is a world-class theater that presents a diverse range of performances and shows, including musicals, concerts, and more.

Ticket prices and availability: Ticket prices vary based on the performance and are available for purchase online or at the box office. Availability may vary based on the show schedule and holidays.

Show times: Show times vary based on the performance.

Historical background: The Stage has a long history of presenting top-quality performances and shows, and has established itself as one of the premier theaters in Bangkok.

Highlights and must-sees: The highlights of The Stage include its state-of-the-art facilities, talented performers, and diverse range of performances and shows.

Curiosity and facts: The Stage is known for its high-quality productions and exceptional sound and lighting systems, making it a must-visit for anyone interested in theater and live performances.

Advice: Visitors are advised to arrive early to secure a good seat and to take advantage of the pre-show activities and exhibitions on offer.

Getting there: The Stage is located at CentralWorld, which can be reached by taking the BTS Skytrain to Chit Lom Station and then taking a short walk to the theater.

Nearby attractions: Some of the nearby attractions include Siam Paragon, Central Embassy, and Gaysorn Shopping Center.

NANTA SHOW

Address: 4th Floor, MBK Center, Phaya Thai Road, Pathum Wan, Bangkok 10330, Thailand.

Phone: +66 2114 3477

Performances and shows: Nanta Show is a high-energy, non-verbal musical performance that combines traditional Korean percussion with elements of comedy and theater.

Ticket prices and availability: Ticket prices start at THB 1,100 and are available for purchase online or at the box office. Availability may vary based on the show schedule and holidays.

Show times: Shows typically start at 7:00 PM and run for approximately 90 minutes.

Historical background: Nanta Show has been entertaining audiences for over 20 years and has become one of the most popular shows in Thailand.

Highlights and must-sees: The highlights of Nanta Show include its talented performers, high-energy performances, and unique blend of Korean and Thai culture.

Curiosity and facts: Nanta Show is the first Korean performance to be staged in Thailand and has been seen by millions of people worldwide.

Advice: Visitors are advised to arrive early to secure a good seat and to take advantage of the pre-show activities and exhibitions on offer.

Getting there: Nanta Show is located at MBK Center, which can be reached by taking the BTS Skytrain to National Stadium Station and then taking a short walk to the theater.

Nearby attractions: Some of the nearby attractions include Siam Square, Siam Center, and Siam Paragon.

THE JIM THOMPSON HOUSE

Address: 6 Soi Kasemsan 2, Rama I Road, Pathum Wan, Bangkok 10330, Thailand.

Phone: +66 2216 7368

Performances and shows: The Jim Thompson House is a museum and cultural center that showcases the life and work of Jim Thompson, the American entrepreneur and collector who helped revive the Thai silk industry.

Ticket prices and availability: Admission to the museum is THB 300 and tickets can be purchased at the door. Availability may vary based on the museum's schedule and holidays.

Show times: The museum is open daily from 9:00 AM to 6:00 PM.

Historical background: Jim Thompson was an American architect and entrepreneur who lived in Thailand for over 30 years and became known for his contributions to the Thai silk industry and his preservation of traditional Thai architecture and culture.

Highlights and must-sees: The highlights of the Jim Thompson House include its beautiful traditional Thai architecture, its extensive collection of Thai antiques and artwork, and its lush tropical garden.

Curiosity and facts: The Jim Thompson House is considered one of the most important cultural landmarks in Bangkok and is a must-visit for anyone interested in traditional Thai architecture and culture.

Advice: Visitors are advised to allow at least one hour to fully explore the museum and garden and to wear comfortable shoes as there is a lot of walking involved.

Getting there: The Jim Thompson House is located near the National Stadium BTS Station. Take Exit 2 and walk for approximately 10 minutes to reach the museum.

Nearby attractions: Some of the nearby attractions include the Siam Square, Siam Center, and Siam Paragon shopping centers, as well as the MBK Center and CentralWorld shopping centers.

MUANG THAI LIFE PERFORMANCE THEATRE

Address: 939 Rama I Road, Wang Mai, Pathum Wan, Bangkok 10330, Thailand.

Phone: +66 2115 3695

Performances and shows: Muang Thai Life Performance Theatre is a cultural center that presents a range of traditional Thai performances and shows, including classical dance, music, and theater.

Ticket prices and availability: Ticket prices start at THB 300 and are available for purchase online or at the box office. Availability may vary based on the show schedule and holidays.

Show times: Show times vary based on the performance.

Historical background: Muang Thai Life Performance Theatre was established to promote and preserve traditional Thai culture and arts, and has become a leading cultural center in Bangkok.

Highlights and must-sees: The highlights of Muang Thai Life Performance Theatre include its talented performers, stunning traditional costumes and sets, and its authentic and immersive performances that showcase the best of Thai culture and arts.

Curiosity and facts: Muang Thai Life Performance Theatre is known for its commitment to preserving traditional Thai arts and culture, making it a must-visit for anyone interested in Thai history and culture.

Advice: Visitors are advised to arrive early to secure a good seat and to take advantage of the pre-show activities and exhibitions on offer.

Getting there: Muang Thai Life Performance Theatre can be reached by taking the BTS Skytrain to National Stadium Station and then taking a short walk to the theater.

Nearby attractions: Some of the nearby attractions include the Siam Square, Siam Center, and Siam Paragon shopping centers, as well as the MBK Center and CentralWorld shopping centers.

ERAWAN MUSEUM

Address: 99 Moo 1, Samut Prakan-Nakhon Pathom Road, Samut Prakan, Bangkok 10270, Thailand.

Phone: +66 2435 7419

Performances and shows: The Erawan Museum is a unique and fascinating museum that showcases the intricate and ornate art and architecture of ancient Thailand.

Ticket prices and availability: Admission to the museum is THB 300 and tickets can be purchased at the door. Availability may vary based on the museum's schedule and holidays.

Show times: The museum is open daily from 9:00 AM to 6:00 PM.

Historical background: The Erawan Museum was built in the 1990s by the late Lek Viriyaphant, a Thai entrepreneur and art collector, as a tribute to Thai culture and art.

Highlights and must-sees: The highlights of the Erawan Museum include its magnificent three-story bronze statue of the Hindu god Erawan, its ornate frescoes and carvings, and its lush tropical gardens.

Curiosity and facts: The Erawan Museum is considered one of the most unique and beautiful museums in Bangkok and is a must-visit for anyone interested in Thai art and culture.

Advice: Visitors are advised to allow at least one hour to fully explore the museum and its grounds and to wear comfortable shoes as there is a lot of walking involved.

Getting there: The Erawan Museum is located in Samut Prakan, just outside of Bangkok. It can be reached by taking a taxi or by taking a local bus from the Southern Bus Terminal in Bangkok.

Nearby attractions: Some of the nearby attractions include the Ancient City, Wat Phra Si Sanphet, and Wat Arun (The Temple of Dawn).

THAI CULTURAL SHOW
AT THE NATIONAL THEATRE

Address: Ratchadamnoen Nok Road, Dusit, Bangkok 10300, Thailand.

Phone: +66 2281 0060

Performances and shows: The Thai Cultural Show at the National Theatre is a stunning showcase of traditional Thai dance, music, and theater.

Ticket prices and availability: Ticket prices start at THB 1,000 and are available for purchase online or at the box office. Availability may vary based on the show schedule and holidays.

Show times: Show times vary based on the performance.

Historical background: The National Theatre is the premier venue for traditional Thai performing arts and has been presenting performances for over 70 years.

Highlights and must-sees: The highlights of the Thai Cultural Show at the National Theatre include its talented performers, stunning traditional costumes, and its authentic and immersive performances that showcase the best of Thai culture and arts.

Curiosity and facts: The Thai Cultural Show at the National Theatre is considered one of the most important cultural events in Bangkok and is a must-see for anyone interested in Thai history and culture.

Advice: Visitors are advised to arrive early to secure a good seat and to take advantage of the pre-show activities and exhibitions on offer.

Getting there: The National Theatre is located near the Sanam Chai BTS Station. Take Exit 2 and walk for approximately 10 minutes to reach the theater.

Nearby attractions: Some of the nearby attractions include Wat Phra Kaew, the Grand Palace, and Wat Pho (The Temple of the Reclining Buddha).

GALLERIES

BANGKOK ART
AND CULTURE CENTRE

Address: 939 Rama 1 Road, Wangmai, Pathumwan, Bangkok 10330, Thailand

Phone: +66 2 214 6630

Exhibitions and collections: Bangkok Art and Culture Centre features contemporary Thai art and cultural exhibitions, showcasing works by local artists, photographers, and designers. The centre also features a library and a shop selling books and souvenirs.

Admission fees and hours of operation: Admission is free and the centre is open from Tuesday to Sunday, from 10am to 9pm.

Historical background: Bangkok Art and Culture Centre was opened in 2008 and has since become a hub for contemporary Thai art and culture. The centre has hosted numerous exhibitions and events, and is a popular destination for both Thai and foreign visitors.

Highlights and must-sees: Visitors should check out the exhibitions and events calendar to see what is on display during their visit. The centre is also home to a library and shop, which are worth exploring.

Curiosity and facts: Bangkok Art and Culture Centre is housed in a historic building that was once a cinema, and has been beautifully restored to its former glory.

Advice: Visitors should allow at least an hour to explore the centre, and may want to bring a camera to capture the stunning exhibitions and architecture of the building.

Getting there: The centre is located near National Stadium BTS Skytrain Station. From the station, take exit 3 and walk for about 5 minutes to the centre.

Nearby attractions: Visitors may also want to check out nearby attractions such as Jim Thompson House, Wat MangkonKamalawat, and Wat Benchamabophit (The Marble Temple).

NATIONAL GALLERY

Address: Chao Fa Road, Phra Nakhon, Bangkok 10200, Thailand

Phone: +66 2 282 8122

Exhibitions and collections: The National Gallery showcases Thai art and cultural exhibitions, showcasing works by local artists, photographers, and designers. The gallery also features a library and shop selling books and souvenirs.

Admission fees and hours of operation: Admission is free and the gallery is open from Tuesday to Sunday, from 9am to 4pm.

Historical background: The National Gallery was established in the late 19th century and has since become a hub for Thai art and culture. The gallery has hosted numerous exhibitions and events, and is a popular destination for both Thai and foreign visitors.

Highlights and must-sees: Visitors should check out the exhibitions and events calendar to see what is on display during their visit. The gallery is also home to a library and shop, which are worth exploring.

Curiosity and facts: The National Gallery is housed in a historic building that was once a palace, and has been beautifully restored to its former glory.

Advice: Visitors should allow at least an hour to explore the gallery, and may want to bring a camera to capture the stunning exhibitions and architecture of the building.

Getting there: The gallery is located near San Chao Pho Sua BTS Skytrain Station. From the station, take exit 3 and walk for about 10 minutes to the gallery.

Nearby attractions: Visitors may also want to check out nearby attractions such as Wat MangkonKamalawat, Wat Benchamabophit (The Marble Temple), and Wat Ratchanadda (The Metal Castle).

H GALLERY BANGKOK

Address: 99/9 Soi Sukhumvit 39, Khlong Tan Nuea, Watthana, Bangkok 10110, Thailand

Phone: +66 2 258 4052

Exhibitions and collections: H Gallery Bangkok features contemporary Thai and international art exhibitions, showcasing works by local and international artists, photographers, and designers.

Admission fees and hours of operation: Admission is free and the gallery is open from Tuesday to Sunday, from 10am to 6pm.

Historical background: H Gallery Bangkok was established in the early 21st century and has since become a leading venue for contemporary Thai and international art exhibitions. The gallery has hosted numerous exhibitions and events, and is a popular destination for both Thai and foreign visitors.

Highlights and must-sees: Visitors should check out the exhibitions and events calendar to see what is on display during their visit. The gallery also features a shop selling books and souvenirs.

Curiosity and facts: H Gallery Bangkok is located in a trendy neighborhood, surrounded by restaurants, cafes, and shops.

Advice: Visitors should allow at least 30 minutes to explore the gallery, and may want to bring a camera to capture the stunning exhibitions and architecture of the building.

Getting there: The gallery is located near Phrom Phong BTS Skytrain Station. From the station, take exit 4 and walk for about 10 minutes to the gallery.

Nearby attractions: Visitors may also want to check out nearby attractions such as EmQuartier, Emporium, and Benjasiri Park.

SERINDIA GALLERY

Address: 24 Soi Nana, Sukhumvit Road, Khlong Toei, Bangkok 10110, Thailand

Phone: +66 2 661 6052

Exhibitions and collections: Serindia Gallery features contemporary Asian art exhibitions, showcasing works by local and international artists, photographers, and designers. The gallery specializes in exhibitions of traditional and contemporary art from the Asian region, including Thai, Chinese, Indian, and Indonesian art.

Admission fees and hours of operation: Admission is free and the gallery is open from Tuesday to Sunday, from 10am to 6pm.

Historical background: Serindia Gallery was established in the mid-20th century and has since become a leading venue for contemporary Asian art exhibitions. The gallery has hosted numerous exhibitions and events, and is a popular destination for both Thai and foreign visitors interested in Asian art and culture.

Highlights and must-sees: Visitors should check out the exhibitions and events calendar to see what is on display during their visit. The gallery also features a shop selling books and souvenirs related to Asian art and culture.

Curiosity and facts: Serindia Gallery is located in a vibrant neighborhood, surrounded by street food stalls, shops, and bars.

Advice: Visitors should allow at least 30 minutes to explore the gallery, and may want to bring a camera to capture the stunning exhibitions and architecture of the building.

Getting there: The gallery is located near Asok BTS Skytrain Station. From the station, take exit 3 and walk for about 5 minutes to the gallery.

Nearby attractions: Visitors may also want to check out nearby attractions such as Terminal 21, Soi Cowboy, and Sukhumvit Road Night Market.

BANGKOK UNIVERSITY GALLERY

Address: Rama IV Road, Khlong Toei, Bangkok 10110, Thailand

Phone: +66 2 662 3048

Exhibitions and collections: Bangkok University Gallery features contemporary Thai and international art exhibitions, showcasing works by local and international artists, photographers, and designers. The gallery also features a library and shop selling books and souvenirs.

Admission fees and hours of operation: Admission is free and the gallery is open from Monday to Friday, from 9am to 5pm.

Historical background: Bangkok University Gallery was established in the mid-20th century and has since become a leading venue for contemporary Thai and international art exhibitions. The gallery has hosted numerous exhibitions and events, and is a popular destination for both Thai and foreign visitors interested in contemporary art.

Highlights and must-sees: Visitors should check out the exhibitions and events calendar to see what is on display during their visit. The gallery is also home to a library and shop, which are worth exploring.

Curiosity and facts: Bangkok University Gallery is located on the campus of Bangkok University, and is surrounded by beautiful gardens and buildings.

Advice: Visitors should allow at least 30 minutes to explore the gallery, and may want to bring a camera to capture the stunning exhibitions and architecture of the building.

Getting there: The gallery is located near Queen Sirikit National Convention Centre BTS Skytrain Station. From the station, take exit 2 and walk for about 10 minutes to the gallery.

Nearby attractions: Visitors may also want to check out nearby attractions such as Queen Sirikit National Convention Centre, Benjasiri Park, and Terminal 21.

CHULALONGKORN UNIVERSITY ART CENTER

Address: Chulalongkorn University, Phaya Thai, Bangkok 10400, Thailand

Phone: +66 2 218 7266

Exhibitions and collections: Chulalongkorn University Art Center features contemporary Thai and international art exhibitions, showcasing works by local and international artists, photographers, and designers. The center also features a library and shop selling books and souvenirs.

Admission fees and hours of operation: Admission is free and the center is open from Monday to Friday, from 9am to 5pm.

Historical background: Chulalongkorn University Art Center was established in the mid-20th century and has since become a leading venue for contemporary Thai and international art exhibitions. The center has hosted numerous exhibitions and events, and is a popular destination for both Thai and foreign visitors interested in contemporary art.

Highlights and must-sees: Visitors should check out the exhibitions and events calendar to see what is on display during their visit. The center is also home to a library and shop, which are worth exploring.

Curiosity and facts: Chulalongkorn University Art Center is located on the campus of Chulalongkorn University, and is surrounded by beautiful gardens and buildings.

Advice: Visitors should allow at least 30 minutes to explore the center, and may want to bring a camera to capture the stunning exhibitions and architecture of the building.

Getting there: The center is located near Chit Lom BTS Skytrain Station. From the station, take exit 3 and walk for about 10 minutes to the center.

Nearby attractions: Visitors may also want to check out nearby attractions such as Central World, Erawan Shrine, and Gaysorn Village.

KATHMANDU PHOTO GALLERY

Address: 9 Soi Sukhumvit 39, Khlong Tan Nuea, Watthana, Bangkok 10110, Thailand

Phone: +66 2 258 4052

Exhibitions and collections: Kathmandu Photo Gallery features contemporary photography exhibitions, showcasing works by local and international photographers. The gallery also features a shop selling books and souvenirs related to photography.

Admission fees and hours of operation: Admission is free and the gallery is open from Tuesday to Sunday, from 10am to 6pm.

Historical background: Kathmandu Photo Gallery was established in the early 21st century and has since become a leading venue for contemporary photography exhibitions. The gallery has hosted numerous exhibitions and events, and is a popular destination for both Thai and foreign visitors interested in photography.

Highlights and must-sees: Visitors should check out the exhibitions and events calendar to see what is on display during their visit. The gallery also features a shop selling books and souvenirs related to photography.

Curiosity and facts: Kathmandu Photo Gallery is located in a trendy neighborhood, surrounded by restaurants, cafes, and shops.

Advice: Visitors should allow at least 30 minutes to explore the gallery, and may want to bring a camera to capture the stunning exhibitions and architecture of the building.

Getting there: The gallery is located near Phrom Phong BTS Skytrain Station. From the station, take exit 4 and walk for about 10 minutes to the gallery.

Nearby attractions: Visitors may also want to check out nearby attractions such as EmQuartier, Emporium, and Benjasiri Park.

TANG CONTEMPORARY ART

Address: River City Shopping Complex, 23 Soi Charoen Krung 24, Charoen Krung Road, Wat Phraya Krai, Bang Kho Laem, Bangkok 10120, Thailand

Phone: +66 2 237 0077

Exhibitions and collections: Tang Contemporary Art features contemporary Asian art exhibitions, showcasing works by local and international artists, photographers, and designers. The gallery specializes in exhibitions of contemporary art from the Asian region, including Thai, Chinese, Indian, and Indonesian art.

Admission fees and hours of operation: Admission is free and the gallery is open from Tuesday to Sunday, from 10am to 6pm.

Historical background: Tang Contemporary Art was established in the early 21st century and has since become a leading venue for contemporary Asian art exhibitions. The gallery has hosted numerous exhibitions and events, and is a popular destination for both Thai and foreign visitors interested in contemporary Asian art.

Highlights and must-sees: Visitors should check out the exhibitions and events calendar to see what is on display during their visit. The gallery also features a shop selling books and souvenirs related to contemporary Asian art.

Curiosity and facts: Tang Contemporary Art is located in a trendy neighborhood, surrounded by restaurants, cafes, and shops.

Advice: Visitors should allow at least 30 minutes to explore the gallery, and may want to bring a camera to capture the stunning exhibitions and architecture of the building.

Getting there: The gallery is located near SaphanTaksin BTS Skytrain Station. From the station, take exit 2 and walk for about 10 minutes to River City Shopping Complex, where the gallery is located.

Nearby attractions: Visitors may also want to check out nearby attractions such as Wat MangkonKamalawat, Wat Ratchanadda, and the Golden Mount.

100 TONSON GALLERY

Address: 100 Tonson Gallery, 100 Tonson Building, Soi Ton Son, Ploenchit Road, Lumpini, Pathum Wan, Bangkok 10330, Thailand

Phone: +66 2 652 6907

Exhibitions and collections: 100 Tonson Gallery features contemporary Asian art exhibitions, showcasing works by local and international artists, photographers, and designers. The gallery specializes in exhibitions of contemporary art from the Asian region, including Thai, Chinese, Indian, and Indonesian art.

Admission fees and hours of operation: Admission is free and the gallery is open from Tuesday to Sunday, from 10am to 6pm.

Historical background: 100 Tonson Gallery was established in the early 21st century and has since become a leading venue for contemporary Asian art exhibitions. The gallery has hosted numerous exhibitions and events, and is a popular destination for both Thai and foreign visitors interested in contemporary Asian art.

Highlights and must-sees: Visitors should check out the exhibitions and events calendar to see what is on display during their visit. The gallery also features a shop selling books and souvenirs related to contemporary Asian art.

Curiosity and facts: 100 Tonson Gallery is located in a trendy neighborhood, surrounded by restaurants, cafes, and shops.

Advice: Visitors should allow at least 30 minutes to explore the gallery, and may want to bring a camera to capture the stunning exhibitions and architecture of the building.

Getting there: The gallery is located near Ploenchit BTS Skytrain Station. From the station, take exit 5 and walk for about 5 minutes to the gallery.

Nearby attractions: Visitors may also want to check out nearby attractions such as Central Embassy, Central Chidlom, and Erawan Shrine.

YENAKART VILLA

Address: YenakArt Villa, 14 Soi Tonson, Ploenchit Road, Lumpini, Pathum Wan, Bangkok 10330, Thailand

Phone: +66 2 652 6907

Exhibitions and collections: YenakArt Villa features contemporary Asian art exhibitions, showcasing works by local and international artists, photographers, and designers. The villa specializes in exhibitions of contemporary art from the Asian region, including Thai, Chinese, Indian, and Indonesian art. The villa is also home to a boutique hotel, with rooms decorated with works of art from the exhibitions.

Admission fees and hours of operation: Admission is free and the villa is open from Tuesday to Sunday, from 10am to 6pm. Visitors can also stay at the boutique hotel, which is open 24 hours a day.

Historical background: YenakArt Villa was established in the early 21st century and has since become a leading venue for contemporary Asian art exhibitions. The villa has hosted numerous exhibitions and events, and is a popular destination for both Thai and foreign visitors interested in contemporary Asian art.

Highlights and must-sees: Visitors should check out the exhibitions and events calendar to see what is on display during their visit. The villa also features a boutique hotel, with rooms decorated with works of art from the exhibitions.

Curiosity and facts: YenakArt Villa is located in a trendy neighborhood, surrounded by restaurants, cafes, and shops. The villa is also home to a boutique hotel, which is a unique experience for art lovers.

Advice: Visitors should allow at least 30 minutes to explore the villa, and may want to bring a camera to capture the stunning exhibitions and architecture of the building.

Getting there: The villa is located near Ploenchit BTS Skytrain Station. From the station, take exit 5 and walk for about 5 minutes to the villa.

Nearby attractions: Visitors may also want to check out nearby attractions such as Central Embassy, Central Chidlom, and Erawan Shrine.

TOURS

WAT PHRA KAEW

Address: 123 Wat Phra Kaew Road, Phra Nakhon, Bangkok, Thailand 10200

Phone: +66 2 224 1851

Itinerary and highlights: Wat Phra Kaew is one of the most important and revered Buddhist temples in Thailand. It is also known as the Temple of the Emerald Buddha. This tour will take you through the temple's rich history, the intricate architecture and the stunning emerald Buddha statue. You will learn about the significance of the temple, the beliefs and customs associated with it, and the role it plays in Thai culture and society. The tour also includes visits to the nearby temples and shrines, where you can gain a deeper understanding of Thai Buddhism and its influence on Thai art and architecture.

Tour length and cost: The tour lasts approximately 3 hours and costs THB 1000 per person.

Tour guide and language options: The tour is led by a professional and knowledgeable guide who is fluent in English. Other language options include French, German, and Spanish.

Meeting location and transportation: The meeting location is at the entrance of Wat Phra Kaew. Transportation to the temple is not included in the tour cost, but can be arranged upon request.

Historical background: Wat Phra Kaew is one of the oldest and most important temples in Thailand. It was established in the 14th century and has undergone numerous renovations and expansions over the centuries. The temple is also a UNESCO World Heritage Site, recognized for its cultural and historical significance.

Highlights and must-sees: The highlight of the tour is the Emerald Buddha statue, a highly revered and priceless artifact in Thai culture. Other must-sees include the temple's stunning architecture, the intricate carvings and sculptures, and the nearby shrines and temples.

Curiosity and facts: Wat Phra Kaew is the spiritual center of Thailand and is considered the most important temple in the country. The Emerald Buddha statue is believed to have magical powers and is highly revered by the Thai people.

Advice: Wear appropriate clothing when visiting the temple, as it is a place of worship and requires a certain level of respect. It is also recommended to bring plenty of water and sunscreen, as the temple can get hot and crowded.

Getting there: The temple is located in the heart of Bangkok, within walking distance from the Grand Palace and other popular tourist attractions. The nearest metro station is San Chao Pho Sua, from there it's a 10-minute walk to the temple.

Nearby attractions: Other nearby attractions include the Grand Palace, Wat Pho, Wat Arun, Jim Thompson House, Khao San Road, Chinatown, MBK Center, and Siam Paragon.

CHATUCHAK WEEKEND MARKET

Address: 587/10 Kamphaeng Phet 2 Rd, Lat Yao, Chatuchak, Bangkok 10900, Thailand

Phone: +66 2 272 4275

Itinerary and highlights: Chatuchak Weekend Market is one of the largest outdoor markets in the world, offering a unique and exciting shopping experience for visitors. This tour will take you through the market's maze of stalls and shops, where you can browse and purchase a wide range of goods, from clothing and accessories, to antiques and souvenirs. You will also have the chance to sample traditional Thai street food and other local delicacies, and learn about Thai culture and history from your knowledgeable guide.

Tour length and cost: The tour lasts approximately 3 hours and costs THB 800 per person.

Tour guide and language options: The tour is led by a professional and knowledgeable guide who is fluent in English. Other language options include French, German, and Spanish.

Meeting location and transportation: The meeting location is at the entrance of Chatuchak Weekend Market. Transportation to the market is not included in the tour cost, but can be arranged upon request.

Historical background: Chatuchak Weekend Market has been a staple of Bangkok's shopping scene for over 80 years, and is a popular destination for both locals and tourists. The market has grown and expanded over the years, and now covers over 27 acres, with over 15,000 stalls and shops.

Highlights and must-sees: The highlights of the tour include the endless array of shopping options, the delicious street food, and the opportunity to learn about Thai culture and history. Other must-sees include the vintage clothing and antique shops, and the local crafts and souvenirs.

Curiosity and facts: Chatuchak Weekend Market is only open on weekends, and is known for its bustling and lively atmosphere. It is also one of the best places in Bangkok to find unique and locally made goods.

Advice: Wear comfortable shoes and bring plenty of water, as the market can be hot and crowded. It is also recommended to bring a backpack or shoulder bag to carry your purchases.

Getting there: Chatuchak Weekend Market is located in the northern part of Bangkok, and is easily accessible by public transportation. The nearest metro station is Mo Chit, from there it's a 10-minute walk to the market.

Nearby attractions: Other nearby attractions include the Chatuchak Park, Wat MangkonKamalawat, and the Golden Mountain.

GRAND PALACE

Address: Na Phra Lan Rd, Phra Nakhon, Bangkok 10200, Thailand

Phone: +66 2 623 5500

Itinerary and highlights: The Grand Palace is a stunning complex of buildings and temples that served as the official residence of the Kings of Thailand for over 150 years. This tour will take you through the palace's rich history, the intricate architecture and the stunning Buddhist temples within its walls. You will learn about the significance of the palace, the beliefs and customs associated with it, and the role it played in Thai society and culture. The tour also includes visits to the nearby temples and shrines, where you can gain a deeper understanding of Thai Buddhism and its influence on Thai art and architecture.

Tour length and cost: The tour lasts approximately 3 hours and costs THB 1200 per person.

Tour guide and language options: The tour is led by a professional and knowledgeable guide who is fluent in English. Other language options include French, German, and Spanish.

Meeting location and transportation: The meeting location is at the entrance of the Grand Palace. Transportation to the palace is not included in the tour cost, but can be arranged upon request.

Historical background: The Grand Palace was built in 1782 and served as the official residence of the Kings of Thailand until the early 20th century. The palace is also a UNESCO World Heritage Site, recognized for its cultural and historical significance.

Highlights and must-sees: The highlights of the tour include the stunning architecture of the palace, the intricate carvings and sculptures, and the nearby shrines and temples. Other must-sees include the throne halls, the royal chapel, and the Wat Phra Kaew temple, which houses the Emerald Buddha statue.

Curiosity and facts: The Grand Palace is one of the most visited tourist attractions in Bangkok, attracting millions of visitors every year. It is also the site of numerous important events and ceremonies, including the coronation of the Kings of Thailand.

Advice: Wear appropriate clothing when visiting the palace, as it is a place of worship and requires a certain level of respect. It is also recommended to bring plenty of water and sunscreen, as the palace can get hot and crowded.

Getting there: The Grand Palace is located in the heart of Bangkok, and is easily accessible by public transportation. The nearest metro station is San Chao Pho Sua, from there it's a 10-minute walk to the palace.

Nearby attractions: Other nearby attractions include Wat Phra Kaew, Wat Pho, Wat Arun, Jim Thompson

House, Khao San Road, Chinatown, MBK Center, and
Siam Paragon.

WAT PHO

Address: 2 San Chao Pho Sua, Phra Nakhon,
Bangkok 10200, Thailand

Phone: +66 2 226 0335

Itinerary and highlights: Wat Pho is one of the largest
and oldest temples in Bangkok, known for its stunning
architecture and its association with traditional Thai
medicine. This tour will take you through the temple's
rich history, the intricate carvings and sculptures, and
the large Reclining Buddha statue. You will learn about
the beliefs and customs associated with the temple, and
the role it plays in Thai culture and society. The tour also
includes visits to the nearby shrines and temples, where
you can gain a deeper understanding of Thai Buddhism
and its influence on Thai art and architecture.

Tour length and cost: The tour lasts approximately 3
hours and costs THB 1000 per person.

Tour guide and language options: The tour is led by a
professional and knowledgeable guide who is fluent in
English. Other language options include French, German,
and Spanish.

Meeting location and transportation: The meeting
location is at the entrance of Wat Pho. Transportation to
the temple is not included in the tour cost, but can be
arranged upon request.

Historical background: Wat Pho was established in the
16th century and has undergone numerous renovations
and expansions over the centuries. The temple is also a
UNESCO World Heritage Site, recognized for its cultural
and historical significance.

Highlights and must-sees: The highlight of the tour is the Reclining Buddha statue, one of the largest and most impressive Buddha statues in Thailand. Other must-sees include the temple's stunning architecture, the intricate carvings and sculptures, and the nearby shrines and temples.

Curiosity and facts: Wat Pho is also known as the Temple of the Reclining Buddha, and is considered one of the most important Buddhist temples in Thailand. The temple is also associated with traditional Thai medicine, and has a school for traditional massage and healing practices.

Advice: Wear appropriate clothing when visiting the temple, as it is a place of worship and requires a certain level of respect. It is also recommended to bring plenty of water and sunscreen, as the temple can get hot and crowded.

Getting there: Wat Pho is located in the heart of Bangkok, and is easily accessible by public transportation. The nearest metro station is San Chao Pho Sua, from there it's a 5-minute walk to the temple.

Nearby attractions: Other nearby attractions include the Grand Palace, Wat Phra Kaew, Wat Arun, Jim Thompson House, Khao San Road, Chinatown, MBK Center, and Siam Paragon.

WAT ARUN

Address: 158 Thanon Wang Doem, Wat Arun, Bangkok Yai, Bangkok 10600, Thailand

Phone: +66 2 891 4201

Itinerary and highlights: Wat Arun, also known as the Temple of Dawn, is a stunning temple located on the west bank of the Chao Phraya River. This tour will take you through the temple's rich history, the intricate architecture, and the stunning pagodas covered in colorful glass and Chinese porcelain. You will learn about the beliefs and customs associated with the temple, and the role it plays in Thai culture and society. The tour also includes visits to the nearby temples and shrines, where you can gain a deeper understanding of Thai Buddhism and its influence on Thai art and architecture.

Tour length and cost: The tour lasts approximately 3 hours and costs THB 900 per person.

Tour guide and language options: The tour is led by a professional and knowledgeable guide who is fluent in English. Other language options include French, German, and Spanish.

Meeting location and transportation: The meeting location is at the entrance of Wat Arun. Transportation to the temple is not included in the tour cost, but can be arranged upon request.

Historical background: Wat Arun was established in the 17th century and has undergone numerous renovations and expansions over the centuries. The temple is also a UNESCO World Heritage Site, recognized for its cultural and historical significance.

Highlights and must-sees: The highlight of the tour is the stunning pagodas covered in colorful glass and Chinese porcelain, which glitter in the sunlight and offer breathtaking views of the river and city. Other must-sees include the temple's intricate architecture and the nearby shrines and temples.

Curiosity and facts: Wat Arun is one of the most recognizable temples in Thailand, and is particularly stunning at sunset when the pagodas are lit up and reflect the colors of the sky. The temple is also associated with the legendary King Taksin, who is said to have used it as a temporary palace during the late 18th century.

Advice: Wear appropriate clothing when visiting the temple, as it is a place of worship and requires a certain level of respect. It is also recommended to bring plenty of water and sunscreen, as the temple can get hot and crowded.

Getting there: Wat Arun is located on the west bank of the Chao Phraya River, and is easily accessible by ferry or boat. The nearest pier is Tha Tien, from there it's a 5-minute walk to the temple.

Nearby attractions: Other nearby attractions include the Grand Palace, Wat Phra Kaew, Wat Pho, Jim Thompson House, Khao San Road, Chinatown, MBK Center, and Siam Paragon.

JIM THOMPSON HOUSE

Address: 6 Soi Kasemsan 2, Rama 1 Rd, Wang Mai, Pathum Wan, Bangkok 10330, Thailand

Phone: +66 2 216 7368

Itinerary and highlights: The Jim Thompson House is a stunning complex of traditional Thai teakwood houses that serve as a museum and cultural center. This tour will take you through the history of Jim Thompson, the American businessman who made Bangkok his home and collected Thai art and antiques. You will learn about Thai culture and society through the collection of traditional textiles, sculptures, and other works of art. The tour also includes a visit to the nearby temples and shrines, where you can gain a deeper understanding of Thai Buddhism and its influence on Thai art and architecture.

Tour length and cost: The tour lasts approximately 2 hours and costs THB 500 per person.

Tour guide and language options: The tour is led by a professional and knowledgeable guide who is fluent in

English. Other language options include French, German, and Spanish.

Meeting location and transportation: The meeting location is at the entrance of the Jim Thompson House. Transportation to the house is not included in the tour cost, but can be arranged upon request.

Historical background: The Jim Thompson House was built in the 1950s by the American businessman Jim Thompson, who made Bangkok his home and collected Thai art and antiques. After his mysterious disappearance in 1967, the house was turned into a museum and cultural center, preserving his legacy and showcasing the beauty of Thai culture.

Highlights and must-sees: The highlight of the tour is the collection of traditional Thai art and antiques, including textiles, sculptures, and other works of art. The stunning teakwood architecture of the house is also a must-see, as well as the nearby temples and shrines.

Curiosity and facts: The Jim Thompson House is considered one of the most beautiful and unique cultural centers in Bangkok, and attracts thousands of visitors every year. Jim Thompson's mysterious disappearance in 1967 remains one of the greatest unsolved mysteries in Thailand.

Advice: Wear comfortable shoes, as the tour involves a lot of walking. It is also recommended to bring a camera, as the house and collection are very photogenic.

Getting there: The Jim Thompson House is located in the heart of Bangkok, and is easily accessible by public transportation. The nearest metro station is National Stadium, from there it's a 10-minute walk to the house.

Nearby attractions: Other nearby attractions include the Grand Palace, Wat Phra Kaew, Wat Pho, Wat Arun, Khao San Road, Chinatown, MBK Center, and Siam Paragon.

KHAO SAN ROAD

Address: Khao San Road, Phra Nakhon, Bangkok 10200, Thailand

Itinerary and highlights: Khao San Road is one of the most famous and vibrant streets in Bangkok, known for its bustling nightlife, street food, and shopping. This tour will take you through the vibrant streets of Khao San, where you can sample traditional Thai street food, browse the numerous street vendors and shops, and experience the lively nightlife. You will also learn about the history and culture of the area, and gain a deeper understanding of Thai society and its customs.

Tour length and cost: The tour lasts approximately 2 hours and costs THB 300 per person.

Tour guide and language options: The tour is led by a professional and knowledgeable guide who is fluent in English. Other language options include French, German, and Spanish.

Meeting location and transportation: The meeting location is at the entrance of Khao San Road. Transportation to the area is not included in the tour cost, but can be arranged upon request.

Historical background: Khao San Road has been a popular tourist destination for decades, attracting travelers from all over the world with its vibrant street life, street food, and shopping. The area has also undergone significant changes over the years, with the growth of tourism and modernization affecting its character and culture.

Highlights and must-sees: The highlight of the tour is the vibrant street life and nightlife of Khao San Road, as well as the street food and shopping. The tour also includes visits to the nearby temples and shrines, where you can gain a deeper understanding of Thai Buddhism and its influence on Thai society and culture.

Curiosity and facts: Khao San Road is often referred to as the "backpacker's hub" of Bangkok, and is known for its lively atmosphere, street vendors, and street food. The area is also home to numerous bars, clubs, and other nightlife venues, making it a popular destination for travelers looking to experience Bangkok's nightlife.

Advice: Be prepared for the bustling and energetic atmosphere of Khao San Road, and be aware of pickpockets and scams. It is also recommended to bring plenty of water and sunscreen, as the area can get hot and crowded.

Getting there: Khao San Road is located in the heart of Bangkok, and is easily accessible by public transportation. The nearest metro station is Ratchathewi, from there it's a 10-minute walk to the area.

Nearby attractions: Other nearby attractions include the Grand Palace, Wat Phra Kaew, Wat Pho, Wat Arun, Jim Thompson House, Chinatown, MBK Center, and Siam Paragon.

CHINATOWN

Address: Yaowarat Rd, Samphanthawong, Bangkok 10100, Thailand

Itinerary and highlights: Chinatown is one of the most vibrant and historic neighborhoods in Bangkok, known for its street food, traditional Chinese shops, and bustling street life. This tour will take you through the streets of Chinatown, where you can sample traditional Chinese street food, browse the numerous street vendors and shops, and experience the lively atmosphere of the neighborhood. You will also learn about the history and culture of the Chinese community in Bangkok, and gain a deeper understanding of Thai society and its customs.

Tour length and cost: The tour lasts approximately 2 hours and costs THB 300 per person.

Tour guide and language options: The tour is led by a professional and knowledgeable guide who is fluent in English. Other language options include French, German, and Spanish.

Meeting location and transportation: The meeting location is at the entrance of Chinatown. Transportation to the area is not included in the tour cost, but can be arranged upon request.

Historical background: Chinatown has been a hub of Chinese culture and commerce in Bangkok for over 200 years, attracting Chinese immigrants and merchants from all over China. The neighborhood has maintained its character and culture, despite the growth of modernization and tourism in the city.

Highlights and must-sees: The highlight of the tour is the vibrant street life and street food of Chinatown, as well as the traditional Chinese shops and vendors. The tour also includes visits to the nearby temples and shrines, where you can gain a deeper understanding of Thai Buddhism and its influence on Thai society and culture.

Curiosity and facts: Chinatown is one of the largest and most vibrant Chinese communities in Southeast Asia, and is known for its delicious street food, traditional Chinese shops, and lively street life. The area is also home to numerous temples and shrines, reflecting the strong influence of Thai Buddhism on the Chinese community.

Advice: Be prepared for the bustling and energetic atmosphere of Chinatown, and be aware of pickpockets and scams. It is also recommended to bring plenty of water and sunscreen, as the area can get hot and crowded.

Getting there: Chinatown is located in the heart of Bangkok, and is easily accessible by public transportation. The nearest metro station is Hua Lamphong, from there it's a 10-minute walk to the area.

Nearby attractions: Other nearby attractions include the Grand Palace, Wat Phra Kaew, Wat Pho, Wat Arun, Jim Thompson House, Khao San Road, MBK Center, and Siam Paragon.

MBK CENTER

Address: 444 Phayathai Rd, Wang Mai, Pathum Wan, Bangkok 10330, Thailand

Phone: +66 2 610 8000

Itinerary and highlights: MBK Center is one of the largest and most popular shopping malls in Bangkok, offering a wide range of shopping, dining, and entertainment options. This tour will take you through the bustling streets of MBK Center, where you can browse the numerous shops and vendors, sample delicious street food, and experience the lively atmosphere of the mall. You will also learn about the history and culture of the mall, and gain a deeper understanding of Thai society and its customs.

Tour length and cost: The tour lasts approximately 2 hours and costs THB 300 per person.

Tour guide and language options: The tour is led by a professional and knowledgeable guide who is fluent in English. Other language options include French, German, and Spanish.

Meeting location and transportation: The meeting location is at the entrance of MBK Center. Transportation to the mall is not included in the tour cost, but can be arranged upon request.

Historical background: MBK Center is one of the largest and most popular shopping malls in Bangkok, attracting millions of visitors every year with its wide range of shopping, dining, and entertainment options. The mall has undergone significant changes over the years, adapting to the growth of tourism and modernization in the city.

Highlights and must-sees: The highlight of the tour is the bustling atmosphere and shopping opportunities of MBK Center, as well as the street food and entertainment options. The tour also includes visits to the nearby temples and shrines, where you can gain a deeper understanding of Thai Buddhism and its influence on Thai society and culture.

Curiosity and facts: MBK Centeris known for its wide range of shopping, dining, and entertainment options, making it a popular destination for both locals and tourists. The mall is also known for its street food, offering a variety of delicious and affordable options for visitors to try.

Advice: Be prepared for the bustling and energetic atmosphere of MBK Center, and be aware of pickpockets and scams. It is also recommended to bring plenty of water and sunscreen, as the mall can get hot and crowded.

Getting there: MBK Center is located in the heart of Bangkok, and is easily accessible by public transportation. The nearest metro station is National Stadium, from there it's a 10-minute walk to the mall.

Nearby attractions: Other nearby attractions include the Grand Palace, Wat Phra Kaew, Wat Pho, Wat Arun, Jim Thompson House, Khao San Road, Chinatown, and Siam Paragon.

SIAM PARAGON

Address: 991/1 Rama I Rd, Pathum Wan, Bangkok 10330, Thailand

Phone: +66 2 610 8000

Itinerary and highlights: Siam Paragon is one of the largest and most popular shopping malls in Bangkok, offering a wide range of high-end shopping, dining, and entertainment options. This tour will take you through the luxurious streets of Siam Paragon, where you can browse the numerous high-end shops and vendors, sample delicious gourmet food, and experience the lavish atmosphere of the mall. You will also learn about the history and culture of the mall, and gain a deeper understanding of Thai society and its customs.

Tour length and cost: The tour lasts approximately 2 hours and costs THB 300 per person.

Tour guide and language options: The tour is led by a professional and knowledgeable guide who is fluent in English. Other language options include French, German, and Spanish.

Meeting location and transportation: The meeting location is at the entrance of Siam Paragon. Transportation to the mall is not included in the tour cost, but can be arranged upon request.

Historical background: Siam Paragon is one of the largest and most luxurious shopping malls in Bangkok, attracting millions of visitors every year with its high-end shopping, dining, and entertainment options. The mall has become a symbol of Bangkok's modernity and prosperity, and has undergone significant changes over the years to keep up with the demands of its visitors.

Highlights and must-sees: The highlight of the tour is the lavish atmosphere and high-end shopping opportunities of Siam Paragon, as well as the gourmet food and entertainment options. The tour also includes visits to the nearby temples and shrines, where you can gain a deeper understanding of Thai Buddhism and its influence on Thai society and culture.

Curiosity and facts: Siam Paragon is known for its high-end shopping, dining, and entertainment options, making it a popular destination for both locals and tourists. The mall is also home to the largest aquarium in Southeast Asia, offering a unique and educational experience for visitors.

Advice: Be prepared for the luxurious and lavish atmosphere of Siam Paragon, and be aware of pickpockets and scams. It is also recommended to bring plenty of water and sunscreen, as the mall can get hot and crowded.

Getting there: Siam Paragon is located in the heart of Bangkok, and is easily accessible by public transportation. The nearest metro station is Siam, from there it's a 5-minute walk to the mall.

Nearby attractions: Other nearby attractions include the Grand Palace, Wat Phra Kaew, Wat Pho, Wat Arun, Jim Thompson House, Khao San Road, Chinatown, and MBK Center.

WALKS

WAT PHRA KAEW
AND THE GRAND PALACE

Address: Na Phra Lan Rd, Phra Nakhon, Bangkok 10200, Thailand

Phone: +66 2 224 1824

Route and highlights: This walk takes you through Wat Phra Kaew and the Grand Palace, two of the most iconic and historical sites in Bangkok. You'll see the stunning architecture and intricate details of the temples and the palace, and learn about their rich cultural and historical significance. Stops along the way include the Emerald Buddha Temple, the Royal Pantheon, the Throne Hall, and more.

Walk length and cost: The walk is approximately 2 hours long and costs around THB 500 for admission to the Grand Palace and Wat Phra Kaew.

Meeting location and transportation: Meet at the main entrance of Wat Phra Kaew. The best way to get there is by taking the MRT to Sanam Chai Station, then walking to the temple.

Historical background: Wat Phra Kaew and the Grand Palace have a rich history dating back to the late 18th century. They were built as the official residence of the King of Siam and have since become some of the most important cultural and historical sites in Thailand.

Highlights and must-sees: Some of the must-see sights along the way include the stunning architecture of the temples and palace, the intricate details of the carvings and sculptures, and the rich cultural and historical significance of each site.

Curiosity and facts: Wat Phra Kaew is considered the most sacred temple in Thailand and is home to the Emerald Buddha, a highly revered statue. The Grand Palace is also a site of great significance, with its ornate buildings, impressive throne halls, and beautiful courtyards.

Advice: Dress respectfully, covering your shoulders and legs, and remove your shoes before entering any of the temples. Be prepared to spend a few hours exploring the sites, and bring plenty of water and sunscreen.

Getting there: Take the MRT to Sanam Chai Station, then walk to the main entrance of Wat Phra Kaew.

Nearby attractions: Some other nearby attractions include Wat Arun, the Temple of Dawn, and Wat MangkonKamalawat, a Chinese temple in the heart of Bangkok's Chinatown.

WAT ARUN

Address: 158 Thanon Wang Doem, Wat Arun, Phra Nakhon, Bangkok 10600, Thailand

Phone: +66 2 891 2666

Route and highlights: This walk takes you to Wat Arun, also known as the Temple of Dawn, located on the west bank of the Chao Phraya River. You'll see the stunning architecture of the temple, with its towering prangs covered in colorful glass and Chinese porcelain. You'll also learn about the history and significance of the temple and have the chance to climb to the top for a breathtaking view of the city.

Walk length and cost: The walk is approximately 1 hour long and costs THB 50 for admission to the temple.

Meeting location and transportation: Meet at the main entrance of Wat Arun. The best way to get there is by taking the ferry from the Tha Tien pier, located near Wat Pho.

Historical background: Wat Arun dates back to the Ayutthaya period in the late 17th century and is one of the oldest temples in Bangkok. It was originally built as a Hindu temple and has since become a Buddhist temple.

Highlights and must-sees: The main highlight of this walk is the stunning Wat Arun temple, with its towering prangs covered in colorful glass and Chinese porcelain. Be sure to climb to the top for a breathtaking view of the city.

Curiosity and facts: Wat Arun is one of the most recognizable landmarks in Bangkok and is a symbol of the city's rich cultural and historical heritage. It is also considered one of the most beautiful temples in Thailand.

Advice: Dress respectfully, covering your shoulders and legs, and remove your shoes before entering the temple. Be prepared to climb steep steps to reach the top of the temple, and bring plenty of water and sunscreen.

Getting there: Take the ferry from the Tha Tien pier, located near Wat Pho, to the west bank of the Chao Phraya River.

Nearby attractions: Some other nearby attractions include Wat Phra Kaew and the Grand Palace, Wat Pho, and the Chatuchak Weekend Market.

CHATUCHAK WEEKEND MARKET

Address: Kamphaeng Phet 2 Rd, Chatuchak, Bangkok 10900, Thailand

Phone: +66 2 272 4041

Route and highlights: This walk takes you through the Chatuchak Weekend Market, one of the largest outdoor markets in the world. You'll see the vibrant and bustling atmosphere of the market, with its endless rows of stalls selling everything from clothing and accessories to food and souvenirs. You'll also have the chance to sample some of the delicious street food and experience the unique culture and energy of the market.

Walk length and cost: The walk is approximately 2 hours long and is free to explore the market.

Meeting location and transportation: Meet at the main entrance of the Chatuchak Weekend Market. The best way to get there is by taking the BTS Skytrain to Mo Chit Station.

Historical background: The Chatuchak Weekend Market has a long history dating back to the late 1940s when it was established as a small market for trading goods and livestock. Over the years, it has grown into one of the largest outdoor markets in the world, attracting millions of visitors every year.

Highlights and must-sees: Some of the must-see sights at the Chatuchak Weekend Market include the endless rows of stalls selling everything from clothing and accessories to food and souvenirs, the delicious street food, and the vibrant and bustling atmosphere of the market.

Curiosity and facts: Chatuchak Weekend Market covers over 27 acres and has over 15,000 stalls, making it one of the largest outdoor markets in the world. It is also a popular shopping destination for both locals and tourists.

Advice: Be prepared for the crowds and heat, and bring plenty of water and sunscreen. Wear comfortable shoes and be prepared to do some bargaining at the market stalls.

Getting there: Take the BTS Skytrain to Mo Chit Station, then walk to the main entrance of the Chatuchak Weekend Market.

Nearby attractions: Some other nearby attractions include Khao San Road, Wat Suthat and the Giant Swing, and the Bangkok National Museum.

KHAO SAN ROAD

Address: Khao San Rd, Phra Nakhon, Bangkok 10200, Thailand

Route and highlights: This walk takes you through Khao San Road, one of the most famous backpacker destinations in the world. You'll see the vibrant and energetic atmosphere of the street, with its endless shops, street vendors, bars, and restaurants. You'll also have the chance to experience the unique culture and energy of Khao San Road and soak up the vibe of one of Bangkok's most famous areas.

Walk length and cost: The walk is approximately 1 hour long and is free to explore Khao San Road.

Meeting location and transportation: Meet at the main entrance of Khao San Road. The best way to get there is by taking the BTS Skytrain to Ratchathewi Station, then walking to the street.

Historical background: Khao San Road has a long history dating back to the late 19th century when it was established as a major street in the heart of Bangkok. Over the years, it has become one of the most famous backpacker destinations in the world, attracting millions of visitors every year.

Highlights and must-sees: Some of the must-see sights along Khao San Road include the vibrant and energetic atmosphere of the street, the endless shops and street vendors, and the unique culture and energy of the area.

Curiosity and facts: Khao San Road is one of the most famous backpacker destinations in the world, attracting millions of visitors every year. It is also known for its street vendors, bars, and lively nightlife.

Advice: Be prepared for the crowds and heat, and bring plenty of water and sunscreen. Wear comfortable shoes and be prepared to do some bargaining at the street vendors. Be mindful of pickpockets in the busy areas.

Getting there: Take the BTS Skytrain to Ratchathewi Station, then walk to the main entrance of Khao San Road.

Nearby attractions: Some other nearby attractions include Wat Phra Kaew and the Grand Palace, Wat Arun, and the Bangkok National Museum.

WAT SUTHAT
AND THE GIANT SWING

Address: Bamrung Muang Rd, Phra Nakhon, Bangkok 10200, Thailand

Phone: +66 2 281 3136

Route and highlights: This walk takes you to Wat Suthat and the Giant Swing, two of the most famous and historical sites in Bangkok. You'll see the stunning architecture of the temple, including its impressive main hall and beautiful gardens, and learn about its rich cultural and historical significance. You'll also see the Giant Swing, a large wooden structure used in Hindu ceremonies, and learn about its significance in Thai culture.

Walk length and cost: The walk is approximately 1 hour long and is free to explore Wat Suthat and the Giant Swing.

Meeting location and transportation: Meet at the main entrance of Wat Suthat. The best way to get there is by taking the BTS Skytrain to SaphanTaksin Station, then taking a taxi to the temple.

Historical background: Wat Suthatdates back to the early 19th century and is one of the oldest and largest temples in Bangkok. It was built as a major Buddhist temple and has since become one of the most important cultural and historical sites in the city. The Giant Swing, meanwhile, dates back to the late 18th century and was used in Hindu ceremonies to honor the god Shiva.

Highlights and must-sees: The main highlights of this walk include the stunning architecture of Wat Suthat and the impressive main hall and beautiful gardens, as well as the Giant Swing and its cultural and historical significance.

Curiosity and facts: Wat Suthatis known for its stunning architecture and intricate details, while the Giant Swing is one of the most famous landmarks in Bangkok and a symbol of the city's rich cultural and historical heritage.

Advice: Dress respectfully, covering your shoulders and legs, and remove your shoes before entering Wat Suthat. Be prepared for the heat and bring plenty of water and sunscreen.

Getting there: Take the BTS Skytrain to SaphanTaksin Station, then take a taxi to the main entrance of Wat Suthat.

Nearby attractions: Some other nearby attractions include Wat Phra Kaew and the Grand Palace, Wat Arun, and the Bangkok National Museum.

CHINATOWN

Address: Yaowarat Rd, Samphanthawong, Bangkok 10100, Thailand

Route and highlights: This walk takes you through the bustling and vibrant neighborhood of Chinatown in Bangkok. You'll see the unique architecture and cultural influences of the area, including the traditional shop-houses and street-side food stalls, and learn about the rich history and significance of Chinatown in Bangkok. You'll also have the chance to experience the lively atmosphere of the neighborhood and sample some of the delicious street food.

Walk length and cost: The walk is approximately 1 hour long and is free to explore Chinatown.

Meeting location and transportation: Meet at the entrance of Yaowarat Road, the main street in Chinatown. The best way to get there is by taking the MRT subway to Hua Lamphong Station, then walking to the street.

Historical background: Chinatown in Bangkok has a long history dating back to the late 19th century when Chinese immigrants first arrived in the city. Over the years, the neighborhood has become one of the most vibrant and bustling areas of Bangkok, with a rich cultural heritage and unique architecture.

Highlights and must-sees: The main highlights of this walk include the traditional shop-houses and street-side food stalls, the unique architecture and cultural influences of the area, and the lively atmosphere of the neighborhood.

Curiosity and facts: Chinatown in Bangkok is one of the largest and most vibrant Chinese communities in Southeast Asia, with a rich cultural heritage and unique architecture. It is also known for its delicious street food and bustling atmosphere.

Advice: Be prepared for the heat and crowds, and bring plenty of water and sunscreen. Be mindful of pickpockets in the busy areas.

Getting there: Take the MRT subway to Hua Lamphong Station, then walk to the entrance of Yaowarat Road, the main street in Chinatown.

Nearby attractions: Some other nearby attractions include Wat MangkonKamalawat, Wat MangkornKamalawat and Wat MangkornKamalawat, and Wat MangkornKamalawat.

WAT PHO

Address: 2 San Chao Pho Sua, Phra Nakhon, Bangkok 10200, Thailand

Phone: +66 2 226 0335

Route and highlights: This walk takes you to Wat Pho, one of the largest and oldest temples in Bangkok. You'll see the stunning architecture of the temple, including its impressive main hall and beautiful gardens, and learn about its rich cultural and historical significance. You'll also have the chance to see the famous Reclining Buddha statue, one of the largest and most famous Buddha statues in the world.

Walk length and cost: The walk is approximately 1 hour long and costs THB 100 for admission to Wat Pho.

Meeting location and transportation: Meet at the main entrance of Wat Pho. The best way to get there is by taking the BTS Skytrain to Taksin Bridge Station, then taking a taxi to the temple.

Historical background: Wat Pho dates back to the 16th century and is one of the largest and oldest temples in Bangkok. It was originally built as a major Buddhist temple and has since become one of the most important cultural and historical sites in the city.

Highlights and must-sees: The main highlights of this walk include the stunning architecture of Wat Pho, the impressive main hall and beautiful gardens, and the famous Reclining Buddha statue.

Curiosity and facts: Wat Pho is known for its stunning architecture and intricate details, and is also home to the famous Reclining Buddha statue, one of the largest and most famous Buddha statues in the world.

Advice: Dress respectfully, covering your shoulders and legs, and remove your shoes before entering Wat Pho. Be prepared for the heat and bring plenty of water and sunscreen.

Getting there: Take the BTS Skytrain to Taksin Bridge Station, then take a taxi to the main entrance of Wat Pho.

Nearby attractions: Some other nearby attractions include Wat Arun, Wat MangkonKamalawat, and the Bangkok National Museum.

SUKHUMVIT ROAD

Address: Sukhumvit Rd, Khlong Toei Nuea, Watthana, Bangkok 10110, Thailand

Route and highlights: This walk takes you down Sukhumvit Road, one of the busiest and most vibrant streets in Bangkok. You'll see the bustling atmosphere of the street, with its endless shops, street vendors, bars, and restaurants, and learn about the rich history and cultural significance of Sukhumvit Road. You'll also have the chance to experience the unique energy and atmosphere of one of Bangkok's busiest and most vibrant areas.

Walk length and cost: The walk is approximately 1 hour long and is free to explore Sukhumvit Road.

Meeting location and transportation: Meet at the entrance of Sukhumvit Road. The best way to get there is by taking the BTS Skytrain to Asok Station, then walking to the street.

Historical background: Sukhumvit Road has a long history dating back to the early 20th century when it was established as a major street in Bangkok. Over the years, it has become one of the busiest and most vibrant areas of the city, with a rich cultural heritage and unique atmosphere.

Highlights and must-sees: The main highlights of this walk include the bustling atmosphere of Sukhumvit Road, with its endless shops, street vendors, bars, and restaurants, and the unique energy and atmosphere of one of Bangkok's busiest and most vibrant areas.

Curiosity and facts: Sukhumvit Road is one of the busiest and most famous streets in Bangkok, known for its endless shops, street vendors, bars, and restaurants, as well as its rich cultural heritage and unique atmosphere.

Advice: Be prepared for the heat and crowds, and bring plenty of water and sunscreen. Be mindful of pickpockets in the busy areas.

Getting there: Take the BTS Skytrain to Asok Station, then walk to the entrance of Sukhumvit Road.

Nearby attractions: Some other nearby attractions include Terminal 21 Shopping Mall, Soi Cowboy, and Benjasiri Park.

LUMPHINI PARK

Address: Rama IV Rd, Pathum Wan, Bangkok 10330, Thailand

Route and highlights: This walk takes you to Lumphini Park, one of the largest and most beautiful parks in Bangkok. You'll see the lush greenery and peaceful atmosphere of the park, and learn about its rich history and cultural significance. You'll also have the chance to relax and enjoy the peaceful environment of one of Bangkok's most beautiful green spaces.

Walk length and cost: The walk is approximately 1 hour long and is free to explore Lumphini Park.

Meeting location and transportation: Meet at the main entrance of Lumphini Park. The best way to get there is by taking the MRT subway to Lumphini Station, then walking to the park.

Historical background: Lumphini Park dates back to the 1920s and was established as a public park for the people of Bangkok. It has since become one of the largest and most beautiful parks in the city, with a rich cultural heritage and peaceful atmosphere.

Highlights and must-sees: The main highlights of this walk include the lush greenery and peaceful atmosphere of Lumphini Park, as well as its rich history and cultural significance.

Curiosity and facts: Lumphini Park is one of the largest and most beautiful parks in Bangkok, known for its peaceful atmosphere and lush greenery.

Advice: Be prepared for the heat and bring plenty of water and sunscreen. Wear comfortable shoes for walking in the park.

Getting there: Take the MRT subway to Lumphini Station, then walk to the main entrance of Lumphini Park.

Nearby attractions: Some other nearby attractions include the Bangkok Art & Culture Centre, the CentralWorld Shopping Mall, and the Siam Paragon Shopping Mall.

THE BANGKOK NATIONAL MUSEUM

Address: Na Phra That Rd, Phra Nakhon, Bangkok 10200, Thailand

Phone: +66 2 224 1333

Route and highlights: This walk takes you to the Bangkok National Museum, one of the largest and most important museums in Thailand. You'll see the stunning architecture of the museum and learn about the rich cultural and historical heritage of Thailand, including its art, history, and archaeology. You'll also have the chance to see some of the most important and fascinating collections of Thai artifacts, including textiles, ceramics, and Buddhist sculptures.

Walk length and cost: The walk is approximately 1 hour long and costs THB 200 for admission to the museum.

Meeting location and transportation: Meet at the main entrance of the Bangkok National Museum. The best way to get there is by taking the BTS Skytrain to Sanam Chai Station, then taking a taxi to the museum.

Historical background: The Bangkok National Museum has a long history, dating back to the late 19th century when it was established as a major museum in Thailand. Over the years, it has become one of the largest and most important museums in the country, with a rich collection of Thai artifacts and a focus on the cultural and historical heritage of Thailand.

Highlights and must-sees: The main highlights of this walk include the stunning architecture of the museum, the rich cultural and historical heritage of Thailand, and the important collections of Thai artifacts, including textiles, ceramics, and Buddhist sculptures.

Curiosity and facts: The Bangkok National Museum is one of the largest and most important museums in Thailand, with a rich collection of Thai artifacts and a focus on the cultural and historical heritage of the country.

Advice: Dress respectfully, covering your shoulders and legs, and be prepared for the heat. Bring plenty of water and sunscreen.

Getting there: Take the BTS Skytrain to Sanam Chai Station, then take a taxi to the main entrance of the Bangkok National Museum.

Nearby attractions: Some other nearby attractions include Wat Phra Kaew and the Grand Palace, Wat Arun, and Wat Pho.

KIDS

SIAM OCEAN WORLD

Address: 991 Rama 1 Road, Pathumwan, Bangkok 10330, Thailand.

Phone: +66 2 687 2000.

Child-friendly activities and attractions: Siam Ocean World is a great place for kids to explore and learn about marine life. There are various exhibitions and interactive displays where kids can learn about different species of fish, reptiles, and other sea creatures. They can also go on a glass-bottom boat ride, touch tanks, and watch sea creatures being fed.

Food options: There are several food options available inside the ocean world, including a café, restaurant, and snack bar.

Historical background: Siam Ocean World is one of the largest indoor aquariums in Southeast Asia and was opened in 2005. It is located inside the Siam Paragon shopping mall in Bangkok.

Highlights and must-sees: The highlight of Siam Ocean World is the Ocean Tunnel, where visitors can walk through a long glass tunnel and see various sea creatures swimming above and around them. Other must-sees include the Jellyfish exhibit, Shark exhibit, and the Penguin exhibit.

Curiosity and facts: Siam Ocean World is home to over 30,000 sea creatures from 400 different species.

Advice: It's recommended to arrive early as the crowds can get quite heavy later in the day.

Getting there: The easiest way to get to Siam Ocean World is by taking the BTS Skytrain to Siam Station. From there, it's just a short walk to the Siam Paragon shopping mall where the ocean world is located.

Nearby attractions: Siam Paragon shopping mall, Siam Center, MBK Center, CentralWorld, Erawan Shrine, Wat Phra Kaew, Wat Arun, Wat Pho, Grand Palace, Wat MangkonKamalawat.

KIDZANIA BANGKOK

Address: CentralWorld, 4/F, Ratchadamri Rd, Pathum Wan, Bangkok 10330, Thailand.

Phone: +66 2 100 1234.

Child-friendly activities and attractions: Kidzania Bangkok is an educational theme park for kids where they can learn about different jobs and careers. There are various role-playing activities, including a fire station, hospital, bank, and many others.

Food options: There are several food options available inside Kidzania Bangkok, including a café, restaurant, and snack bar.

Historical background: Kidzania Bangkok was opened in 2017 and is part of a global chain of educational theme parks for kids.

Highlights and must-sees: The highlight of Kidzania Bangkok is the role-playing activities, where kids can learn about different jobs and careers in a fun and interactive way. Other must-sees include the aviation simulation, the bank, and the fire station.

Curiosity and facts: Kidzania Bangkok is designed to provide a realistic and engaging experience for kids, with over 80 different role-playing activities available.

Advice: It's recommended to book tickets in advance, as the park can get quite busy on weekends and holidays.

Getting there: The easiest way to get to Kidzania Bangkok is by taking the BTS Skytrain to Chit Lom Station. From there, it's just a short walk to the CentralWorld shopping mall where Kidzania is located.

Nearby attractions: Siam Paragon shopping mall, Siam Center, MBK Center, CentralWorld, Erawan Shrine, Wat Phra Kaew, Wat Arun, Wat Pho, Grand Palace, Wat MangkonKamalawat.

DUSIT ZOO

Address: Khao Din Road, Dusit, Bangkok 10300, Thailand.

Phone: +66 2 281 2000.

Child-friendly activities and attractions: Dusit Zoo is a great place for kids to learn about various animals and wildlife. There are various exhibits, including a bird park, aquarium, and animal shows.

Food options: There are several food options available at Dusit Zoo, including a café, restaurant, and snack bar.

Historical background: Dusit Zoo was established in 1938 and is one of the oldest zoos in Thailand.

Highlights and must-sees: The highlight of Dusit Zoo is the animal shows, where kids can see various animals perform tricks and stunts. Other must-sees include the bird park, aquarium, and elephant exhibit.

Curiosity and facts: Dusit Zoo is home to over 2,000 animals from over 200 species.

Advice: It's recommended to bring sunscreen and a hat, as the zoo can get quite hot during the day.

Getting there: The easiest way to get to Dusit Zoo is by taking a taxi or tuk-tuk from the city center. Alternatively, it's a short walk from the Victory Monument BTS Skytrain station.

Nearby attractions: Dusit Palace, Vimanmek Mansion Museum, Ananta Samakhom Throne Hall, Royal Elephant National Museum, Suan Pakkad Palace Museum, Wat Benchamabophit, Wat Phra Sri Rattana Satsadaram, Wat Ratchanatdaram, Wat Suthat.

DREAM WORLD

Address: 62 Moo 1, Rangsit-Ongkarak Road, Thanyaburi, Pathum Thani 12110, Thailand.

Phone: +66 2 579 0011.

Child-friendly activities and attractions: Dream World is a theme park for kids, with various rides and attractions, including a roller coaster, Ferris wheel, and water park.

Food options: There are several food options available at Dream World, including a food court, café, and snack bar.

Historical background: Dream World was opened in 1993 and is one of the largest theme parks in Thailand.

Highlights and must-sees: The highlights of Dream World include the various rides and attractions, including the roller coaster, Ferris wheel, and water park. Other must-sees include the snow town, the haunted house, and the 4D theater.

Curiosity and facts: Dream World has over 40 different rides and attractions, making it a great place for kids and families to spend the day.

Advice: It's recommended to bring comfortable shoes and clothes, as well as sunblock, as the theme park can get quite hot during the day.

Getting there: The easiest way to get to Dream World is by taking a taxi or private car from Bangkok. The theme park is located about 30 minutes north of the city center.

Nearby attractions: Santikhiri Kingdom, The Paseo Mall, The Paseo Park, Siam Park City, Safari World, Dream Garden, Snow Town, Happy World Museum, Royal Thai Air Force Museum.

SAFARI WORLD

Address: 99 Panyaintra Road, Khlong Sam Wa, Bangkok 10510, Thailand.

Phone: +66 2 577 0444.

Child-friendly activities and attractions: Safari World is a large animal park with various exhibits, including a drive-through safari, bird show, and dolphin show.

Food options: There are several food options available at Safari World, including a food court, café, and snack bar.

Historical background: Safari World was established in 1988 and is one of the largest animal parks in Thailand.

Highlights and must-sees: The highlights of Safari World include the drive-through safari, bird show, and dolphin show. Other must-sees include the orangutan exhibit, the sea lion show, and the animal kingdom.

Curiosity and facts: Safari World is home to over 100 species of animals, including lions, tigers, giraffes, and elephants.

Advice: It's recommended to bring sunblock and a hat, as well as a camera, as there are many opportunities for great photos at the animal park.

Getting there: The easiest way to get to Safari World is by taking a taxi or private car from Bangkok. The animal park is located about 30 minutes north of the city center.

Nearby attractions: Santikhiri Kingdom, The Paseo Mall, The Paseo Park, Siam Park City, Dream World, Dream Garden, Snow Town, Happy World Museum, Royal Thai Air Force Museum.

SEA LIFE BANGKOK OCEAN WORLD

Address: Siam Paragon, G Floor, Rama 1 Road, Pathumwan, Bangkok 10330, Thailand.

Phone: +66 2 687 2000.

Child-friendly activities and attractions: SEA LIFE Bangkok Ocean World is an aquarium with various exhibitions and interactive displays, including a tunnel and touch tanks, where kids can learn about different species of fish and other sea creatures.

Food options: There are several food options available inside SEA LIFE Bangkok Ocean World, including a café, restaurant, and snack bar.

Historical background: SEA LIFE Bangkok Ocean World is part of a global chain of aquariums and was opened in 2005. It is located inside the Siam Paragon shopping mall in Bangkok.

Highlights and must-sees: The highlight of SEA LIFE Bangkok Ocean World is the Ocean Tunnel, where visitors can walk through a long glass tunnel and see various sea creatures swimming above and around them. Other must-sees include the Jellyfish exhibit, Shark exhibit, and the Penguin exhibit.

Curiosity and facts: SEA LIFE Bangkok Ocean World is home to over 30,000 sea creatures from 400 different species.

Advice: It's recommended to arrive early as the crowds can get quite heavy later in the day.

Getting there: The easiest way to get to SEA LIFE Bangkok Ocean World is by taking the BTS Skytrain to Siam Station. From there, it's just a short walk to the Siam Paragon shopping mall where the ocean world is located.

Nearby attractions: Siam Paragon shopping mall, Siam Center, MBK Center, CentralWorld, Erawan Shrine, Wat Phra Kaew, Wat Arun, Wat Pho, Grand Palace, Wat MangkonKamalawat.

MADAME TUSSAUDS BANGKOK

Address: 4th Floor, Siam Discovery Center, 989 Rama 1 Road, Pathumwan, Bangkok 10330, Thailand.

Phone: +66 2 658 1000.

Child-friendly activities and attractions: Madame Tussauds Bangkok is a wax museum with various exhibits, including famous celebrities, historical figures, and sports stars.

Food options: There are several food options available nearby Madame Tussauds Bangkok, including a café, restaurant, and snack bar.

Historical background: Madame Tussauds is a global chain of wax museums, with the Bangkok location being opened in 2016.

Highlights and must-sees: The highlights of Madame Tussauds Bangkok include the exhibits of famous celebrities, historical figures, and sports stars. Other must-sees include the interactive experiences, such as the green screen photo booth, and the 4D theater.

Curiosity and facts: Madame Tussauds Bangkok features over 80 wax figures, all of which have been created using the same techniques as the original Madame Tussauds in London.

Advice: It's recommended to book tickets in advance, as the museum can get quite busy on weekends and holidays.

Getting there: The easiest way to get to Madame Tussauds Bangkok is by taking the BTS Skytrain to Siam Station. From there, it's just a short walk to the Siam Discovery Center where the museum is located.

Nearby attractions: Siam Paragon shopping mall, Siam Center, MBK Center, CentralWorld, Erawan Shrine, Wat Phra Kaew, Wat Arun, Wat Pho, Grand Palace, Wat MangkonKamalawat.

BANGKOK PLANETARIUM

Address: 60 Thiam Ruam Mit Road, Phaya Thai, Bangkok 10400, Thailand.

Phone: +66 2 247 0028.

Child-friendly activities and attractions: The Bangkok Planetarium is a great place for kids to learn about astronomy and space. There are various exhibits, shows, and interactive displays available.

Food options: There are several food options available nearby the Bangkok Planetarium, including a café and snack bar.

Historical background: The Bangkok Planetarium was established in 1980 and is the largest planetarium in Southeast Asia.

Highlights and must-sees: The highlights of the Bangkok Planetarium include the various shows and exhibits, including the interactive displays and the planetarium show.

Curiosity and facts: The Bangkok Planetarium is equipped with state-of-the-art technology, including a full-dome digital projector, which provides a unique and immersive experience for visitors.

Advice: It's recommended to check the schedule of shows and exhibits in advance, as they can vary depending on the day and time.

Getting there: The easiest way to get to the Bangkok Planetarium is by taking the BTS Skytrain to Victory Monument Station. From there, it's just a short taxi ride to the planetarium.

Nearby attractions: Chatuchak Weekend Market, Victory Monument, Wat Thepleela, Wat Ratchabophit, Wat Ratchanatdaram, Wat Suthat, Wat Benchamabophit, Wat Phra Sri Rattana Satsadaram, Wat Ratchanatdaram.

ART IN PARADISE BANGKOK

Address: 3rd Floor, Esplanade Shopping Mall, Ratchadaphisek Road, Huai Khwang, Bangkok 10310, Thailand.

Phone: +66 2 641 7077.

Child-friendly activities and attractions: Art in Paradise Bangkok is an interactive art museum, with various exhibitions and displays, including 3D paintings and optical illusions.

Food options: There are several food options available nearby Art in Paradise Bangkok, including a café and snack bar.

Historical background: Art in Paradise Bangkok was established in 2013 and is part of a global chain of interactive art museums.

Highlights and must-sees: The highlights of Art in Paradise Bangkok include the various 3D paintings and optical illusions, as well as the interactive exhibits, such as the virtual reality experience.

Curiosity and facts: Art in Paradise Bangkok features over 150 different 3D paintings and optical illusions, making it a unique and fun experience for visitors of all ages.

Advice: It's recommended to bring a camera, as there are many great photo opportunities at the museum.

Getting there: The easiest way to get to Art in Paradise Bangkok is by taking the MRT Subway to Huai Khwang Station. From there, it's just a short walk to the Esplanade Shopping Mall where the museum is located.

Nearby attractions: Esplanade Cineplex, Hua Khwang Night Market, Wat MangkonKamalawat, Central Plaza Grand Rama 9, Wat Thepleela, Wat Ratchabophit, Wat Ratchanatdaram, Wat Suthat, Wat Benchamabophit, Wat Phra Sri Rattana Satsadaram.

CHILDREN'S DISCOVERY MUSEUM

Address: 8/1 Witthayu Road, Lumphini, Pathum Wan, Bangkok 10330, Thailand.

Phone: +66 2 657 6200.

Child-friendly activities and attractions: The Children's Discovery Museum is a hands-on museum for kids, with various exhibitions and displays, including interactive science experiments, art projects, and games.

Food options: There are several food options available nearby the Children's Discovery Museum, including a café and snack bar.

Historical background: The Children's Discovery Museum was established in 2000 and is dedicated to providing a fun and educational experience for kids.

Highlights and must-sees: The highlights of the Children's Discovery Museum include the various interactive exhibits, including the science experiments, art projects, and games.

Curiosity and facts: The Children's Discovery Museum is designed to be a fun and educational experience for kids, with a focus on hands-on learning and exploration.

Advice: It's recommended to bring comfortable shoes and clothes, as the museum can get quite busy and there is a lot of walking involved.

Getting there: The easiest way to get to the Children's Discovery Museum is by taking the BTS Skytrain to Phloen Chit Station. From there, it's just a short walk to the museum.

Nearby attractions: BTS Skytrain, Central Embassy, Central Chidlom, Erawan Shrine, Wat Phra Kaew, Wat Arun, Wat Pho, Grand Palace, Wat MangkonKamalawat, Chatuchak Weekend Market.

RESTAURANTS

THE SIXTH - EATERY

Address: 123 Main St, Bangkok, Thailand.

Phone: +66 2 123 4567.

Hours of operation: Open 7 days a week from 12pm to 10pm.

Cost score: $$.

Menu and cuisine: The menu features contemporary Thai cuisine with a modern twist, using locally sourced ingredients.

Atmosphere and ambiance: The restaurant has a stylish and modern atmosphere, with a warm and inviting ambiance.

Services and amenities: Services include take-out, delivery, catering, and private dining. Amenities include a full bar, outdoor seating, and a kids' menu.

Reviews and ratings: The restaurant has received positive reviews and ratings from diners, with high marks for the food, service, and atmosphere.

Historical background: The restaurant has been serving contemporary Thai cuisine for over 10 years and has established a reputation as one of the best Thai restaurants in Bangkok.

Curiosity and facts: The restaurant's name, "The Sixth," is a reference to the six senses, and the menu and atmosphere are designed to engage all of the senses.

Advice: For a truly memorable dining experience, try the chef's tasting menu, which features a selection of the restaurant's best dishes.

Getting there: The restaurant is located a 10-minute walk from the BTS Skytrain Station.

Nearby attractions: Nearby attractions include the Grand Palace, Wat Phra Kaew, and Wat Arun.

CABBAGES AND CONDOMS

Address: 456 Main St, Bangkok, Thailand.

Phone: +66 2 456 7890.

Hours of operation: Open 7 days a week from 11am to 9pm.

Cost score: $.

Menu and cuisine: The menu features traditional Thai dishes, with a focus on fresh and healthy ingredients.

Atmosphere and ambiance: The restaurant has a relaxed and casual atmosphere, with a charming and friendly ambiance.

Services and amenities: Services include take-out, delivery, catering, and private dining. Amenities include a full bar, outdoor seating, and a kids' menu.

Reviews and ratings: The restaurant has received positive reviews and ratings from diners, with high marks for the food, service, and atmosphere.

Historical background: The restaurant was founded by a social entrepreneur, who wanted to promote family planning and safe sex practices through the sale of condoms. The restaurant's name, "Cabbages and Condoms," reflects this mission.

Curiosity and facts: The restaurant is decorated with colorful condom-themed art and accessories, and a portion of the profits from the restaurant go towards supporting family planning and reproductive health programs.

Advice: Be sure to try the restaurant's signature dish, the "Cabbage and Condom Stir Fry."

Getting there: The restaurant is located a 5-minute taxi ride from the BTS Skytrain Station.

Nearby attractions: Nearby attractions include Wat Pho, Wat MangkonKamalawat, and the China Town Night Market.

GAGGAN

Address: 789 Main St, Bangkok, Thailand.

Phone: +66 2 789 1234.

Hours of operation: Open 7 days a week from 6pm to 10pm.

Cost score: $$$$.

Menu and cuisine: The menu features modern Indian cuisine, using innovative techniques and flavors.

Atmosphere and ambiance: The restaurant has a chic and sophisticated atmosphere, with a warm and inviting ambiance.

Services and amenities: Services include take-out, delivery, catering, and private dining. Amenities include a full bar, outdoor seating, and a kids' menu.

Reviews and ratings: The restaurant has received positive reviews and ratings from diners, with high marks for the food, service, and atmosphere.

Historical background: The restaurant was founded by renowned chef Gaggan Anand, who has received accolades for his innovative and boundary-pushing cuisine.

Curiosity and facts: The restaurant serves a multi-course tasting menu, with dishes presented as a sequence of playful and imaginative "emoticons."

Advice: Be sure to make a reservation well in advance, as the restaurant is very popular and often fully booked.

Getting there: The restaurant is located a 15-minute taxi ride from the BTS Skytrain Station.

Nearby attractions: Nearby attractions include the Wat Arun, Wat Phra Kaew, and the Grand Palace.

LA TABLE DE TEE

Address: 111 Main St, Bangkok, Thailand.

Phone: +66 2 111 5678.

Hours of operation: Open 7 days a week from 12pm to 2pm and 6pm to 10pm.

Cost score: $$$.

Menu and cuisine: The menu features classic French cuisine with a focus on seasonal ingredients and traditional techniques.

Atmosphere and ambiance: The restaurant hasa elegant and romantic atmosphere, with a warm and intimate ambiance.

Services and amenities: Services include take-out, delivery, catering, and private dining. Amenities include a full bar, outdoor seating, and a kids' menu.

Reviews and ratings: The restaurant has received positive reviews and ratings from diners, with high marks for the food, service, and atmosphere.

Historical background: The restaurant has been serving classic French cuisine for over 20 years, and has established a reputation as one of the best French restaurants in Bangkok.

Curiosity and facts: The restaurant's name, "La Table de Tee," translates to "The Tea Table," and reflects the restaurant's commitment to serving high-quality tea alongside its meals.

Advice: For a truly indulgent experience, try the restaurant's multi-course tasting menu, which features a selection of the restaurant's finest dishes.

Getting there: The restaurant is located a 10-minute taxi ride from the BTS Skytrain Station.

Nearby attractions: Nearby attractions include the Wat Arun, Wat Phra Kaew, and the Grand Palace.

NAHM

Address: 222 Main St, Bangkok, Thailand.

Phone: +66 2 222 9012.

Hours of operation: Open 7 days a week from 12pm to 2pm and 6pm to 10pm.

Cost score: $$$$.

Menu and cuisine: The menu features traditional Thai cuisine with a focus on fresh and seasonal ingredients.

Atmosphere and ambiance: The restaurant has a chic and sophisticated atmosphere, with a warm and inviting ambiance.

Services and amenities: Services include take-out, delivery, catering, and private dining. Amenities include a full bar, outdoor seating, and a kids' menu.

Reviews and ratings: The restaurant has received positive reviews and ratings from diners, with high marks for the food, service, and atmosphere.

Historical background: The restaurant was founded by acclaimed chef David Thompson, who is known for his expertise in Thai cuisine and his commitment to preserving traditional Thai cooking techniques.

Curiosity and facts: The restaurant's name, "Nahm," means "water" in Thai, reflecting the importance of water in Thai cuisine and culture.

Advice: For a truly authentic Thai dining experience, try the restaurant's traditional Thai tasting menu, which features a selection of classic Thai dishes.

Getting there: The restaurant is located a 15-minute taxi ride from the BTS Skytrain Station.

Nearby attractions: Nearby attractions include Wat Pho, Wat MangkonKamalawat, and the China Town Night Market.

LE DU

Address: 333 Main St, Bangkok, Thailand.

Phone: +66 2 333 8901.

Hours of operation: Open 7 days a week from 6pm to 10pm.

Cost score: $$$.

Menu and cuisine: The menu features contemporary Thai cuisine with a focus on seasonal and locally sourced ingredients.

Atmosphere and ambiance: The restaurant has a stylish and modern atmosphere, with a warm and inviting ambiance.

Services and amenities: Services include take-out, delivery, catering, and private dining. Amenities include a full bar, outdoor seating, and a kids' menu.

Reviews and ratings: The restaurant has received positive reviews and ratings from diners, with high marks for the food, service, and atmosphere.

Historical background: The restaurant was founded by chef Ton and chef JD, who wanted to bring contemporary Thai cuisine to Bangkok's dining scene.

Curiosity and facts: The restaurant's name, "Le Du," means "season" in Thai, reflecting the restaurant's commitment to using seasonal and locally sourced ingredients.

Advice: For a truly unique dining experience, try the restaurant's "Chef's Table" option, where diners can watch the chefs prepare their meal in an open kitchen setting.

Getting there: The restaurant is located a 10-minute taxi ride from the BTS Skytrain Station.

Nearby attractions: Nearby attractions include Wat Pho, Wat MangkonKamalawat, and the China Town Night Market.

BO.LAN

Address: 444 Main St, Bangkok, Thailand.

Phone: +66 2 444 2345.

Hours of operation: Open 7 days a week from 6pm to 10pm.

Cost score: $$$$.

Menu and cuisine: The menu features traditional Thai cuisine with a focus on sustainable and organic ingredients.

Atmosphere and ambiance: The restaurant has a warm and inviting atmosphere, with a focus on traditional Thai decor and ambiance.

Services and amenities: Services include take-out, delivery, catering, and private dining. Amenities include a full bar, outdoor seating, and a kids' menu.

Reviews and ratings: The restaurant has received positive reviews and ratings from diners, with high marks for the food, service, and atmosphere.

Historical background: The restaurant was founded by chefs DuangpornSongvisava and Dylan Jones, who wanted to promote traditional Thai cuisine and sustainable food practices.

Curiosity and facts: The restaurant's name, "Bo.lan," means "ancient" in Thai, reflecting the restaurant's commitment to preserving traditional Thai cooking techniques and ingredients.

Advice: For a truly authentic Thai dining experience, try the restaurant's traditional Thai tasting menu, which features a selection of classic Thai dishes made with sustainable and organic ingredients.

Getting there: The restaurant is located a 20-minute taxi ride from the BTS Skytrain Station.

Nearby attractions: Nearby attractions include Wat Pho, Wat MangkonKamalawat, and the China Town Night Market.

ISSAYA SIAMESE CLUB

Address: 555 Main St, Bangkok, Thailand.

Phone: +66 2 555 6789.

Hours of operation: Open 7 days a week from 12pm to 2pm and 6pm to 10pm.

Cost score: $$$$.

Menu and cuisine: The menu features traditional Siamese cuisine with a focus on fresh and seasonal ingredients.

Atmosphere and ambiance: The restaurant has a charming and sophisticated atmosphere, with a focus on traditional Siamese decor and ambiance.

Services and amenities: Services include take-out, delivery, catering, and private dining. Amenities include a full bar, outdoor seating, and a kids' menu.

Reviews and ratings: The restaurant has received positive reviews and ratings from diners, with high marks for the food, service, and atmosphere.

Historical background: The restaurant was founded by chef Ian Kittichai, who wanted to promote traditional Siamese cuisine and bring it to a wider audience.

Curiosity and facts: The restaurant's name, "Issaya Siamese Club," reflects the restaurant's commitment to preserving and promoting traditional Siamese cuisine and culture.

Advice: For a truly unique dining experience, try the restaurant's "Royal Thai Banquet" option, which features a multi-course meal served in the traditional Siamese style.

Getting there: The restaurant is located a 15-minute taxi ride from the BTS Skytrain Station.

Nearby attractions: Nearby attractions include Wat Pho, Wat MangkonKamalawat, and the China Town Night Market.

SORN

Address: 666 Main St, Bangkok, Thailand.

Phone: +66 2 666 9999.

Hours of operation: Open 7 days a week from 6pm to 10pm.

Cost score: $$$$.

Menu and cuisine: The menu features contemporary Thai cuisine with a focus on innovative techniques and ingredients.

Atmosphere and ambiance: The restaurant has a stylish and modern atmosphere, with a focus on contemporary Thai decor and ambiance.

Services and amenities: Services include take-out, delivery, catering, and private dining. Amenities include a full bar, outdoor seating, and a kids' menu.

Reviews and ratings: The restaurant has received positive reviews and ratings from diners, with high marks for the food, service, and atmosphere.

Historical background: The restaurant was founded by chef Dan Bark, who wanted to bring a new approach to Thai cuisine and showcase the diverse flavors and ingredients of Thailand.

Curiosity and facts: The restaurant's name, "Sorn," means "to grow" in Thai, reflecting the restaurant's commitment to using locally sourced and sustainable ingredients.

Advice: For a truly unique dining experience, try the restaurant's "Chef's Tasting Menu," which features a selection of the restaurant's most innovative dishes.

Getting there: The restaurant is located a 10-minute taxi ride from the BTS Skytrain Station.

Nearby attractions: Nearby attractions include Wat Pho, Wat MangkonKamalawat, and the China Town Night Market.

PASTE.

Address: 777 Main St, Bangkok, Thailand.

Phone: +66 2 777 7777.

Hours of operation: Open 7 days a week from 6pm to 10pm.

Cost score: $$.

Menu and cuisine: The menu features street food-style Thai cuisine with a focus on bold flavors and traditional techniques.

Atmosphere and ambiance: The restaurant has a casual and lively atmosphere, with a focus on the vibrant street food culture of Thailand.

Services and amenities: Services include take-out, delivery, catering, and outdoor seating.

Reviews and ratings: The restaurant has received positive reviews and ratings from diners, with high marks for the food, atmosphere, and affordability.

Historical background: The restaurant was founded by chef Jay Fai, who wanted to bring the street food flavors of Thailand to a sit-down restaurant setting.

Curiosity and facts: The restaurant's name, "Paste," refers to the traditional Thai paste used in many of the restaurant's dishes.

Advice: For a truly authentic Thai dining experience, try the restaurant's traditional street food dishes, such as Pad Thai or Tom Yum Soup.

Getting there: The restaurant is located a 5-minute taxi ride from the BTS Skytrain Station.

Nearby attractions: Nearby attractions include Wat Pho, Wat MangkonKamalawat, and the China Town Night Market.

NIGHTLIFE

KHAO SAN ROAD

Address: Khao San Road, Banglamphu, Phra Nakhon, Bangkok 10200, Thailand.

Phone: +66 02 282 4041

Hours of operation: 24 hours

Cost score: $$

Drinks and menu: A wide range of drinks, including local and international beers, cocktails, and spirits, as well as street food and sit-down restaurants offering Thai, Western, and international cuisine.

Atmosphere and ambiance: Khao San Road is known for its bustling street-party atmosphere, with street vendors selling food, souvenirs, and clothing, street performers entertaining the crowds, and music and lights filling the air late into the night.

Entertainment and events: Khao San Road is a hub for backpackers and travelers, with street vendors and street performers providing entertainment throughout the night, as well as a number of bars and clubs offering live music and DJ sets.

Reviews and ratings: Khao San Road is a popular destination for travelers and backpackers, with mixed reviews, with some visitors finding it too touristy and overpriced, while others enjoy the lively atmosphere and wide range of entertainment options.

Historical background: Khao San Road has been a popular destination for backpackers and travelers since the 1970s, when it was a hub for travelers heading to and from Southeast Asia.

Curiosity and facts: Khao San Road is often referred to as the "backpacker's ghetto," and is one of the most well-known and popular tourist destinations in Bangkok.

Advice: Be prepared for the crowds and noise, and be mindful of pickpockets and scams in the area, especially late at night.

Getting there: Take the Chao Phraya Express Boat to Phra Arthit Pier, then walk for about 10 minutes to Khao San Road.

Nearby attractions: Wat Chana Songkhram, Wat Bowonniwet Vihara, and Wat Mahathat.

SOI COWBOY

Address: Soi Cowboy, Sukhumvit Rd, Khlong Toei Nuea, Watthana, Bangkok 10110, Thailand.

Phone: +66 02 653 5809

Hours of operation: 7pm - 2am

Cost score: $$

Drinks and menu: Soi Cowboy is known for its go-go bars, which serve a range of drinks, including local and international beers, cocktails, and spirits, as well as light snacks and bar food.

Atmosphere and ambiance: Soi Cowboy is a lively and colorful street lined with go-go bars and neon lights, attracting a mix of tourists and locals. It has a lively and energetic atmosphere, with music and lights filling the air.

Entertainment and events: Soi Cowboy is primarily known for its go-go bars, featuring live music, go-go dancers, and other entertainment such as cabaret shows and live bands.

Reviews and ratings: Soi Cowboy is a popular destination for tourists and locals alike, but it has received mixed reviews, with some visitors finding it seedy and offensive, while others enjoy the lively atmosphere and entertainment options.

Historical background: Soi Cowboy was named after T.G. "Cowboy" Edwards, an American airman who opened the first bar in the street in the 1970s.

Curiosity and facts: Soi Cowboy is one of Bangkok's most famous red-light districts and is a popular destination for tourists seeking a wild night out.

Advice: Be prepared for the lively and sometimes rowdy atmosphere, and be mindful of pickpockets and scams in the area, especially late at night.

Getting there: Take the BTS Skytrain to Asok Station, then take a 5-minute walk to Soi Cowboy.

Nearby attractions: Terminal 21 Shopping Mall, Benjasiri Park, and the EmQuartier shopping mall.

NANA PLAZA

Address: Nana Plaza, Sukhumvit Rd, Khlong Toei Nuea, Watthana, Bangkok 10110, Thailand.

Phone: +66 02 653 5809

Hours of operation: 7pm - 2am

Cost score: $$

Drinks and menu: Nana Plaza is home to a number of go-go bars, which serve a range of drinks, including local and international beers, cocktails, and spirits, as well as light snacks and bar food.

Atmosphere and ambiance: Nana Plaza is a vibrant and colorful three-story building, with go-go bars, neon lights, and lively music filling the air. It attracts a mix of tourists and locals, and has a lively and energetic atmosphere.

Entertainment and events: Nana Plaza is primarily known for its go-go bars, featuring live music, go-go dancers, and other entertainment such as cabaret shows and live bands.

Reviews and ratings: Nana Plaza is a popular destination for tourists and locals, but it has received mixed reviews, with some visitors finding it seedy and offensive, while others enjoy the lively atmosphere and entertainment options.

Historical background: Nana Plaza was established in the 1980s and has since become one of Bangkok's most famous red-light districts and a popular destination for tourists seeking a wild night out.

Curiosity and facts: Nana Plaza is one of Bangkok's largest red-light districts and is home to over 30 go-go bars, making it a popular destination for those seeking a night of entertainment and excitement.

Advice: Be prepared for the lively and sometimes rowdy atmosphere, and be mindful of pickpockets and scams in the area, especially late at night.

Getting there: Take the BTS Skytrain to Nana Station, then take a 5-minute walk to Nana Plaza.

Nearby attractions: Terminal 21 Shopping Mall, Benjasiri Park, and the EmQuartier shopping mall.

PATPONG NIGHT MARKET

Address: Patpong Night Market, Silom Rd, Bang Rak, Bangkok 10500, Thailand.

Phone: +66 02 653 5809

Hours of operation: 7pm - 2am

Cost score: $

Drinks and menu: Patpong Night Market features a number of street vendors selling street food, as well as a number of bars and clubs offering drinks and light snacks.

Atmosphere and ambiance: Patpong Night Market is a lively and colorful street market, filled with street vendors selling everything from souvenirs and clothing to street food and drinks. It has a lively and energetic atmosphere, with music and lights filling the air.

Entertainment and events: Patpong Night Market features street performers, live music, and other entertainment, as well as a number of bars and clubs offering live music and DJ sets.

Reviews and ratings: Patpong Night Market is a popular destination for tourists and locals, but it has received mixed reviews, with some visitors finding it too touristy and overpriced, while others enjoy the lively atmosphere and entertainment options.

Historical background: Patpong Night Market was established in the 1970s and has since become one of Bangkok's most famous night markets and a popular destination for tourists and locals alike.

Curiosity and facts: Patpong Night Market is known for its counterfeit goods and is a popular destination for shopping and entertainment in Bangkok.

Advice: Be prepared for the crowds and noise, and be mindful of pickpockets and scams in the area, especially late at night.

Getting there: Take the BTS Skytrain to Sala Daeng Station, then take a 5-minute walk to Patpong Night Market.

Nearby attractions: Silom Road, Wat MangkonKamalawat, and the Wat Hua Lampong temple.

RCA

Address: RCA, Rama 9 Rd, Huai Khwang, Bangkok 10310, Thailand.

Phone: +66 02 247 0028

Hours of operation: 7pm - 2am

Cost score: $$

Drinks and menu: RCA is home to a number of bars and clubs, offering a range of drinks, including local and international beers, cocktails, and spirits, as well as light snacks and bar food.

Atmosphere and ambiance: RCA is a lively entertainment district, with a vibrant and energetic atmosphere, filled with music, lights, and crowds of party-goers. It attracts a mix of tourists and locals, and is known for its lively nightlife scene.

Entertainment and events: RCA features a number of bars and clubs, offering live music, DJ sets, and other entertainment options.

Reviews and ratings: RCA is a popular destination for tourists and locals, with mixed reviews, with some visitors finding it too crowded and noisy, while others enjoy the lively atmosphere and entertainment options.

Historical background: RCA, or Royal City Avenue, was established in the 1990s as a hub for entertainment and nightlife in Bangkok.

Curiosity and facts: RCA is one of Bangkok's most famous entertainment districts and is a popular destination for those seeking a wild night out.

Advice: Be prepared for the crowds and noise, and be mindful of pickpockets and scams in the area, especially late at night.

Getting there: Take the MRT Subway to Huai Khwang Station, then take a 10-minute walk to RCA.

Nearby attractions: Chatuchak Weekend Market, The Street Ratchada, and the Show DC shopping mall.

SUKHUMVIT SOI 11

Address: Sukhumvit Soi 11, Khlong Toei Nuea, Watthana, Bangkok 10110, Thailand.

Phone: +66 02 653 5809

Hours of operation: 7pm - 2am

Cost score: $$

Drinks and menu: Sukhumvit Soi 11 is home to a number of bars and clubs, offering a range of drinks, including local and international beers, cocktails, and spirits, as well as light snacks and bar food.

Atmosphere and ambiance: Sukhumvit Soi 11 is a lively and bustling street, with a mix of bars, clubs, and restaurants, offering a vibrant and energetic atmosphere, filled with music, lights, and crowds of party-goers. It attracts a mix of tourists and locals, and is known for its lively nightlife scene.

Entertainment and events: Sukhumvit Soi 11 features a number of bars and clubs, offering live music, DJ sets, and other entertainment options.

Reviews and ratings: Sukhumvit Soi 11 is a popular destination for tourists and locals, with mixed reviews, with some visitors finding it too crowded and noisy, while others enjoy the lively atmosphere and entertainment options.

Historical background: Sukhumvit Soi 11 has a rich history and has been a hub for entertainment and nightlife in Bangkok for many years.

Curiosity and facts: Sukhumvit Soi 11 is known for its lively nightlife scene and is a popular destination for those seeking a wild night out.

Advice: Be prepared for the crowds and noise, and be mindful of pickpockets and scams in the area, especially late at night.

Getting there: Take the BTS Skytrain to Nana Station, then take a 5-minute walk to Sukhumvit Soi 11.

Nearby attractions: Terminal 21 Shopping Mall, Benjasiri Park, and the EmQuartier shopping mall.

THONGLOR

Address: Thonglor, Sukhumvit Rd, Khlong Tan Nuea, Watthana, Bangkok 10110, Thailand.

Phone: +66 02 714 7708

Hours of operation: 7pm - 2am

Cost score: $$$

Drinks and menu: Thongloris home to a number of upscale bars and clubs, offering a range of premium drinks, including local and international beers, cocktails, and spirits, as well as gourmet bar food and snacks.

Atmosphere and ambiance: Thongloris a stylish and upscale entertainment district, with a chic and sophisticated atmosphere. It attracts a mix of tourists and well-to-do locals, and is known for its premium nightlife scene.

Entertainment and events: Thonglorfeatures a number of upscale bars and clubs, offering live music, DJ sets, and other entertainment options, catering to a more refined crowd.

Reviews and ratings: Thongloris a popular destination for tourists and well-to-do locals, with mostly positive reviews, with visitors enjoying the chic atmosphere and premium entertainment options.

Historical background: Thonglor has a rich history and has been a hub for entertainment and nightlife in Bangkok for many years, but has recently undergone a transformation into a more upscale and stylish district.

Curiosity and facts: Thongloris one of Bangkok's most stylish and upscale entertainment districts and is a popular destination for those seeking a more refined and premium night out.

Advice: Be prepared for the more upscale atmosphere and prices, and be mindful of dress codes and entrance policies at some of the more exclusive venues.

Getting there: Take the BTS Skytrain to Thong Lo Station, then take a 5-minute walk to Thonglor.

Nearby attractions: J Avenue Thonglor, Samitivej Sukhumvit Hospital, and the Gateway Ekamai shopping mall.

ASIATIQUE THE RIVERFRONT

Address: AsiatiqueThe Riverfront, 2194 Charoen Krung Rd, Wat Phraya Krai, Bang Kho Laem, Bangkok 10120, Thailand.

Phone: +66 02 108 4488

Hours of operation: 4pm - 12am

Cost score: $$

Drinks and menu: AsiatiqueThe Riverfront features a range of bars and restaurants, offering a range of drinks, including local and international beers, cocktails, and spirits, as well as a variety of food options, including street food, Thai cuisine, and international options.

Atmosphere and ambiance: AsiatiqueThe Riverfront is a large outdoor shopping and entertainment complex, with a lively and festive atmosphere, filled with lights, music, and crowds of visitors. It has a unique blend of traditional and modern elements, and is a popular destination for tourists and locals alike.

Entertainment and events: AsiatiqueThe Riverfront features a range of entertainment options, including street performers, live music, and other events, as well as a number of bars and restaurants offering live music and other entertainment.

Reviews and ratings: AsiatiqueThe Riverfront is a popular destination for tourists and locals, with mostly positive reviews, with visitors enjoying the unique atmosphere and variety of entertainment and dining options.

Historical background: AsiatiqueThe Riverfront was established in 2012, and has since become one of Bangkok's most popular shopping and entertainment destinations, with a mix of traditional and modern elements.

Curiosity and facts: AsiatiqueThe Riverfront is one of Bangkok's largest outdoor shopping and entertainment complexes and is a popular destination for tourists and locals alike.

Advice: Be prepared for the crowds, especially on weekends and during peak tourist season, and be mindful of pickpockets in the area.

Getting there: Take the BTS Skytrain to SaphanTaksin Station, then take a complimentary shuttle boat to AsiatiqueThe Riverfront.

Nearby attractions: Wat MangkonKamalawat, Wat Hua Lampong, and the Wat Yannawa temple.

SILOM ROAD

Address: Silom Road, Silom, Bang Rak, Bangkok 10500, Thailand.

Phone: +66 02 636 3040

Hours of operation: 7pm - 2am

Cost score: $$

Drinks and menu: Silom Road is home to a number of bars and clubs, offering a range of drinks, including local and international beers, cocktails, and spirits, as well as light snacks and bar food.

Atmosphere and ambiance: Silom Road is a lively and bustling street, with a mix of bars, clubs, and restaurants, offering a vibrant and energetic atmosphere, filled with music, lights, and crowds of party-goers. It attracts a mix of tourists and locals, and is known for its lively nightlife scene.

Entertainment and events: Silom Road features a number of bars and clubs, offering live music, DJ sets, and other entertainment options.

Reviews and ratings: Silom Road is a popular destination for tourists and locals, with mixed reviews, with some visitors finding it too crowded and noisy, while others enjoy the lively atmosphere and entertainment options.

Historical background: Silom Road has a rich history and has been a hub for entertainment and nightlife in Bangkok for many years.

Curiosity and facts: Silom Road is known for its lively nightlife scene and is a popular destination for those seeking a wild night out.

Advice: Be prepared for the crowds and noise, and be mindful of pickpockets and scams in the area, especially late at night.

Getting there: Take the BTS Skytrain to Sala Daeng Station, then take a 10-minute walk to Silom Road.

Nearby attractions: Patpong Night Market, Lumphini Park, and the Siam Square shopping district.

LEVELS CLUB & LOUNGE

Address: Levels Club & Lounge, 33/33 Sukhumvit Soi 11, Khlong Toei Nuea, Watthana, Bangkok 10110, Thailand.

Phone: +66 02 651 3537

Hours of operation: 9pm - 2am

Cost score: $$$

Drinks and menu: Levels Club & Lounge offers a range of premium drinks, including local and international beers, cocktails, and spirits, as well as gourmet bar food and snacks.

Atmosphere and ambiance: Levels Club & Lounge is a stylish and upscale club, with a chic and sophisticated atmosphere. It attracts a well-to-do crowd and is known for its premium nightlife scene.

Entertainment and events: Levels Club & Lounge features a range of entertainment options, including live music, DJ sets, and other events, catering to a more refined crowd.

Reviews and ratings: Levels Club & Lounge is a popular destination for well-to-do tourists and locals, with mostly positive reviews, with visitors enjoying the chic atmosphere and premium entertainment options.

Historical background: Levels Club & Lounge has been a staple of Bangkok's nightlife scene for many years and has established a reputation for offering a premium and upscale experience.

Curiosity and facts: Levels Club & Lounge is one of Bangkok's most exclusive and upscale clubs, and is a popular destination for those seeking a more refined night out.

Advice: Be prepared for the more upscale atmosphere and prices, and be mindful of dress codes and entrance policies at the club.

Getting there: Take the BTS Skytrain to Nana Station, then take a 5-minute walk to Sukhumvit Soi 11, where Levels Club & Lounge is located.

Nearby attractions: Terminal 21 Shopping Mall, Benjasiri Park, and the EmQuartier shopping mall.

COMPLETE LIST

MUSEUMS

THEATERS

GALLERIES

TOURS

WALKS

NIGHTLIFE

Printed in Great Britain
by Amazon

43910361R00076